THE STRAIGHT TRUTH
The Life of an Expert Witness

Written By William Gulya
Edited by Vivien Kooper

First published by Dog Ear Publishing
4010 W. 86th Street, Ste H
Indianapolis, IN 46268
www.dogearpublishing.net

ISBN: 978-145750-670-3

This book is printed on acid-free paper.

Printed in the United States of America

Acknowledgments

It is strange to think that I have been working non-stop for forty years, and this is my first book. The desire to harness my knowledge and expertise, and use it to help others, was the catalyst that made me finally take on this endeavor.

First and foremost, I want to thank Kathy, my loving and understanding wife of thirty-seven years, who has always been my inspiration to excel and succeed.

To my children, William and Stacy... You have made me proud to be your father, blessed me with four wonderful grandchildren, and supported my efforts in creating this book.

I want to thank my office manager, Jennifer Gasper. I have watched you blossom over the years, as you went from being my receptionist to my right arm.

Special thanks must go to Rosalie Hamilton, without whose guidance and mentoring my expert witness and consulting practice may never have existed.

Very special thanks and appreciation must go to my talented and patient editor, Vivien Kooper, who understood my message, and whose hard work and dedication to this book allowed it to become a reality.

I want to thank Diane McKenna, who took the raw vision for the book cover and turned it into a work of art.

I would also like to thank all the authors of the books I have read and studied. They have been an invaluable source of inspiration and guidance to me. The knowledge and wisdom they put into their books will continue to educate and inspire me—and many others—for years to come.

Last, but not least, I would like to thank Ashford University for professors and curriculum that have provided me with the highest degree of education. Collectively, they have honed my reasoning, writing, and professional skills, so that I could become one of the best, and better serve my clients.

Disclaimer

The purpose of this book is to entertain and educate. Neither author nor publisher shall have liability or responsibility to any person or entity, with respect to any loss or damage caused, or alleged to be caused, directly or indirectly, by the information contained herein.

This book has been developed to provide information and insights related to the subject matter contained within. It is sold and distributed with the understanding that neither author nor publisher is engaging in providing legal advice, or other professional advice. If legal or other professional services are required, the reader should seek the services of a competent professional.

It is not the intent of this book to reprint all the information that is otherwise available to the reader. Rather, it is the author's intent to share his personal experiences, and to complement, supplement, and expound on other available text and resources.

Every effort has been made to make this book as accurate and complete as possible. However, there may be typographical and/or content-based errors contained herein; and there may be certain examples and guidance that have been overstated or exaggerated for purposes of entertainment, emphasis, and effect. Therefore, this book should be used only as a general guide.

This book contains *typical* questions and answers. However, each expert's field of expertise is different—as is every jurisdiction, situation, strategy, client, and attorney. Therefore, the reader will not want to use, verbatim, all the answers or guidance provided.

Please note that the word "he" is used consistently throughout this book. This was done for purposes of simplicity only, and is not meant to indicate gender bias. Expert witnesses may be either male or female.

Lastly, please keep in mind that laws and philosophies will change. The author cannot predict how, when, or to what extent laws, court rules, or rulings may change, during or after the writing and publishing of this book.

Anyone who does not agree with the above may return this book for a full refund.

Introduction

So, why would you want to become an expert witness?

After all, the work can be very tedious and demanding. It can require the expenditure of long hours for two, three, or even four weeks at a time.

You will be under extreme pressure to meet deadlines from retaining counsel—and opposing counsel will look for, and seize upon, every opportunity to attack your credibility. While you are being deposed by opposing counsel, everything you have ever done will seemingly become fair game.

Your opinions will be questioned. Opposing counsel will attempt to pick you apart. Attorneys may even belittle you on the witness stand.

Throughout it all, you will have to remain calm, composed, and professional.

In light of everything I've mentioned, let me repeat the question—why would you want to become an expert witness?

The answer lies within each individual...

You may have years of extensive experience in a particular field.

You may have extensive education in a particular field or industry.

✸You may be looking for additional income.

You may be looking to retire, and seeking to put your experience to good use.

You may enjoy the excitement of helping to determine, and even alter, the course of people's lives.

You may find it satisfying to affect the award and distribution of large sums of money.

You may relish the challenge of proving, or disproving, best practices or industry standards in your field.

You may want to help ensure that justice is served.

Or, you may simply enjoy the chance to make a difference.

Whatever your qualifying reason, working as an expert witness can be extremely rewarding—both financially and mentally.

While I am unaware of published data about expert witness fees (experts are sometimes reluctant to publish their annual income), I know that fees can range from $50.00 to $800.00 per hour, or more, depending on their field of expertise. A successful expert can earn $100,000.00 per year, or more.

In fact, a highly sought-after expert in his or her field can almost name their fee. After all, when the retaining counsel has a case where millions of dollars are at stake, winning the case takes precedence over any concerns about the expert's fee.

One reason for the good earning potential: Expert witness practices have relatively low overhead requirements. In terms of equipment, you will need a good computer with data backup system, color scanner, internet connection, website (preferably professionally built), phone, pencils, pens, pads, paper clips, and other stationery supplies. That's about it.

You won't need to incur office expenses; you can work out of your home.

On those occasions when you are required to travel out of town or out of state, travel expenses related to hotels, airfare, and rental cars are paid either by retaining counsel or opposing counsel.

✳✳Very few other businesses offer such a low overhead with such a potentially lucrative return.

Expert witness work is a growing occupation. It has been said, "The cost may be high to employ the expert, but it may well be higher *not* to employ one. Indeed, counsel who chooses to proceed without an expert may be flirting with malpractice." (Melvin Belli Sr., Trial Magazine)

Table of Contents

"Do you swear to tell the truth,
the whole truth,
and nothing but the truth,
so help you God?"

~ 1 ~
EXPERIENCE
The Expert's Most Valuable Asset

"The young man knows the rules,
but the old man knows the exceptions."
~Oliver Wendell Holmes

• Making a Difference

I have been in the business of site-work construction since I was a kid. I started out working for my father and uncles during summer vacations, went full-time in 1972, and eventually took over my father's business. I have been quite successful, but the reality is that my line of work is limited, in terms of the kind of fulfillment it offers.

Like a painting that starts with a blank canvas, we start with an unimproved piece of land. *Unlike* the creation of a painting, my work generally goes unnoticed. No one remembers what the land looked like before we started, so there is little appreciation of the hard work we did to mold and shape it. Nobody ever sees the pipes underground, or fully understands what it takes to shape the earth, and make the parking lots.

Building construction is different. People might watch a building going up and say, "Gee, that's a nice looking building!" Rarely does anyone ever look at a parking lot and say, "Gee, that's a great looking parking lot!" It happens only once in a blue moon.

Every working person wants to feel that the contribution they make in their particular line of work has an impact, and adds value in the greater scheme of life.

The idea of becoming an expert witness began to appeal to me because I saw it as a way to truly make a difference—in a way that people could easily recognize and understand.

An expert witness is described as follows (quoted from the online encyclopedia, www.wikipedia.org):

"An expert witness, professional witness, or judicial witness is a witness who, by virtue of education, training, skill, or experience is believed to have expertise and specialized knowledge in a particular subject beyond that of the average person, sufficient that others may sufficiently and legally rely upon the witness's specialized (scientific, technical, or other) opinion about an evidence or fact issue within the scope of his expertise, referred to as the expert opinion, as an assistance to the fact-finder. Expert witnesses may also deliver expert evidence from the domain of their expertise..."

All you have to do is look at that definition, and you can begin to see how being an expert witness offers the opportunity to be of service to others in a very concrete and meaningful way.

Expert work always leads to a tangible result. And, it all begins with your report. Your expert witness report is a critical part of the judicial process, and is often a major factor in determining whether or not a case ever goes to trial. More cases settle than not, due in large part to the presence of expert witnesses in the judicial process. In fact, of the 15,000,000 lawsuits filed each year, 95% are settled out of court.

If a case does proceed to court, the expert's report has a huge impact on how the jury absorbs the evidence and facts. A well-constructed, well-written report ensures that the jury will give due consideration to the expert's opinions and conclusion related to the evidence and facts at issue in the case.

Prior to any trial, your report will be submitted to opposing counsel, as part of the discovery process. Once you, as the expert witness, take the stand in a courtroom, or are deposed in deposition, the opposing counsel will attempt to twist, manipulate, and take out of context the contents of your report. It's nothing personal. It's their job, and it is worthy of respect.

But, at the end of the day, attorneys know what they're up against. For all their posturing, they realize that an expert opinion supported by the facts, the evidence, *and the truth*, is irrefutable.

Does that mean that the truth always wins out in the end, and justice is served in every case? Sadly, no.

It does mean that an expert witness properly doing their job, and telling the truth, the whole truth, and nothing but the truth as they know it to be, can profoundly alter the direction of a case.

In the ideal scenario, the opinions and conclusion expressed by the expert will motivate opposing counsel to go to their client and say, "You know, we potentially have problems in this case that will be very difficult to overcome. If we address these things by battling it out in a court of law, my fee is going to be hundreds of dollars per hour. When you multiply my hourly fee times each eight-hour day we spend in court, the costs can add up. Maybe we ought to think about getting this matter resolved."

When your expert report is instrumental in inducing settlement, you can't help but feel like you're making a real difference.

• Assessing Your Qualifications

Once I had decided I was potentially interested in becoming an expert witness, I had to determine whether I could turn my knowledge and experience into something that would help others with their legal issues. Some honest self-assessment was in order. I had to ask myself some hard questions, and be willing to hear the answers.

The very first question I needed to ask myself was this: Am I qualified to be an expert witness? If the answer to that question was no, there would be no point in giving the idea any further consideration.

What was the main qualification of any expert witness? Experience.

First and foremost, I needed to be experienced, and know my field thoroughly. I needed to have experienced many different circumstances and situations, and know the proper, industry accepted way to handle them.

- **Reviewing Your Experience**

I was born in Perth Amboy, New Jersey, and began my life in Fords, a small suburb. The entire town occupied no more than one square mile.

I have one sibling—a sister, four years younger than I am. My mother was a stay-at-home mom, as was the custom among women of that era.

My father had his own construction company, and was in business for himself. Dad had a way about him, and everybody loved him. He was the kind of guy who would give you the shirt off his back. Sadly, he would die at the young age of sixty-one, due to causes unrelated to his work.

The idea of following my father into the construction business did not appeal to me. I wanted to be an architect, and entered college with that in mind. Midway through my schooling, I took a summer internship as a draftsman at a small company. I quickly discovered that being an architect was better in theory than in practice. It definitely wasn't for me.

Working for my father was the quickest, easiest way for me to get work.

At that time, my father's construction company was very small. He employed no more than four or five workers. They had to make do with a small dump truck and a couple of backhoes. That was pretty much the extent of the equipment fleet in those days. My dad used the local deli as his office, and he always arrived at "the office" armed with plenty of change for the payphone on the wall.

As I mentioned, even as a young boy, I was exposed to the construction business. My father was always up, and out of the house, before I left for school. When I hit twelve or thirteen, I started doing odd jobs on the weekends and during summer vacations, for Dad's construction company—and others.

My uncle had a residential sheetrock business and, for a couple of summers, he put me to work, spotting nails with spackle. Another one of my uncles was a home builder, and put me to work, cleaning up the houses after his construction crews.

I found construction work to be far more interesting than working as a draftsman, due to the simple fact that every workday was a little bit different. So, I was always learning something new.

As a draftsman, I was doing more or less the same thing every day. The designs would differ, but the process, and the concepts, were always the same.

When paydays rolled around, I would join the rest of my father's crew at the deli. My dad would ask us, "So, how many hours did you work this week?" We would write down our hours on napkins we pulled from the napkin holder. Needless to say, our system was very informal.

I had a feeling I could do better. It was a gut instinct that told me I could take my father's business in directions he hadn't even dreamed possible. It's hard to say where a young guy came up with that kind of confidence, but there you have it.

I was on my way. I set out to grow my father's business in every way possible. My vision was for us to gain more clients, employ more workers, and institute formal methods of recording costs, payroll, and time expenditures. None of this would happen overnight. I would start at the bottom and work my way up.

I began as a laborer and assistant and, as I learned more, I was able to do more and more on my own. It wasn't long before I was laying out the jobs, and operating the equipment.

As it turned out, my architecture schooling came in handy. I could already read blueprints. Not only that, but most of my coursework focused on *civil* architecture, where the focus was on designing the earth and the site—a perfect match for my father's site-work construction business. (By contrast, the focus of building architecture and mechanical engineering has to do with structures and buildings.)

Speaking of buildings, my father's company bought a piece of property. And, through a fortuitous twist of fate, we ended up with an office.

Here's what happened: We were working for a company that hired us to demolish a metal shed, measuring approximately twenty-five by fifty feet. I took one look at the shed, and saw the future offices of our construction company. So, rather than demolishing it, I dismantled it, piece by piece, and bolt by bolt, and reconstructed it on my father's new property.

We had our first building office and shop—and not only had we not had to pay a penny for it, we had in fact been paid to acquire it! My father neither objected to, nor applauded, this ingenuity. He merely accepted it. Dad had faith in my abilities, and didn't think to question my choices.

Dad's company worked for mechanical contractors. We would dig, backfill, and restore whatever surface we were dealing with, so that the mechanical contractor could do their work, which included the installation of underground piping.

In the early years of his business, my father worked primarily for one client. Having all our eggs in one basket seemed to me like a risky way to do business. More importantly, I felt that diversification was the fastest way to grow our company. So, I began soliciting work from various companies, and bidding on their jobs that related to site work. I knocked on doors and made cold calls, asking to be included on the bidders' lists of various companies.

All I had in my arsenal was a scale/ruler, a pad of paper, a pencil, and a Casio calculator. I sat behind my plywood desk, poring over the blueprints, and estimating the jobs. I would figure out how many cubic yards of dirt we had to move, and how many lengths of underground pipe we were going to need. Once I had calculated the costs of a job, I would submit the bid—on one of the first computer models ever made by Apple.

Company after company accepted our bid, and gave us the job. One thing led to another, and Dad gave me free rein to run with my ideas.

By 1980, I found myself in charge of the business.

My father's health was beginning to deteriorate. He had a condition that required monthly visits to the doctor. Then he had a stroke—followed by a heart attack. As I mentioned, my father was a wonderful man, beloved by everyone, so everyone was saddened to see his health decline. By the time Dad was taken down by a heart attack, he was the boss in name only. I was already running the company.

After Dad's passing (God rest his soul), I inherited ownership interest in the business. I essentially took a one-client company to a point where we were doing, at our peak, $12,000,000.00 to $20,000,000.00 worth of contracts per year. We went from four employees to sixty, and from three or four pieces of equipment to forty.

During the years that followed 1972, many things transpired, some more memorable than others. Suffice it to say that, with nearly forty years of experience in the site-work construction industry, I was exceptionally qualified to become an expert witness in that field.

~ 2 ~
PERSPECTIVE
Considering the Expert Life

"It's not what you look at that matters.
It's what you see."
~Henry David Thoreau

• Utilizing Skills Acquired Along the Way

I already knew that I had decades of experience in site-work construction that could potentially enable me to become an effective and sought-after expert witness. But, I also realized that knowing how to dig a trench according to OSHA standards and regulations, shore a trench according to best practices, and operate heavy equipment, was not going to help me very much if I didn't possess the other necessary qualities.

I needed a well-rounded perspective on the undertaking I was considering.

I began to consider other aspects of the expert witness life. The more I contemplated my decision, the more the big picture came into view.

I could see how my construction experience had made me imminently qualified to opine on matters related to my industry, taught me valuable lessons that would come in very handy in my expert witness practice, and given me skills that would translate well to my new business life.

One of the most important lessons I ever learned was taught to me early in life by my father's father. Grandpa was a carpenter by trade. In the days following the end of World War II, he would go to the army depot, pick up wooden ammunition crates they were throwing away, and use them to build homes.

He told me, "Do it right, or don't do it at all. When you cut a board, measure twice, cut once! Or else, every time you cut it, it will be too short!"

His words would echo in my ears throughout my lifetime. "Measure twice, cut once!" Be thorough. Be sure. Do everything in your power to avoid making mistakes that will ultimately cost you.

I also remembered various incidents that had arisen in the course of doing business, and realized how the skills I had acquired along the way could be applied in my new role.

I would never forget writing the estimate for what would turn out to be my first million-dollar-plus job. At that time, it was a huge bid for us. When we were awarded the project, I was filled with nervous enthusiasm. I wanted to make absolutely sure we were prepared for the job.

Did we have the proper equipment? Sufficient manpower? I had to make sure I could purchase the right materials at the right price. I needed to pay attention to progress and productivity, and never lose sight of the bottom line. We were going to need substantial financial backing to even begin the job. It was time to get a credit line.

This taught me about the importance of preparation.

I also remembered times when, regardless of how well prepared we were, there were things that went wrong. That is always true in the field of construction.

The weather is one great example of forces beyond our control that can, from time to time, profoundly impact a project. One good string of bad weather would significantly skew our well-planned budget. I remembered times when it was raining cats and dogs, and it was impossible for the workers to begin or complete a job. Regardless of whether our workers were out there working hard and sweating in the hot sun, or standing around unable to work due to inclement weather, we were still required to pay them.

Even when the sun was shining high in the sky, and we couldn't have asked for better weather, there were times when we ran into some impediment below ground. We had to contend with underground obstructions not shown on drawings and specs. Sometimes, site conditions differed from the drawings. Or, we received change orders which put a whole new slant on the job.

Whenever we found ourselves stuck with conditions and circumstances we had been unable to anticipate and prepare for, I thought to myself, *Your job is to solve the problem and stop the bleeding.*

How? By remaining analytical and ready to think on my feet.

From early on, my motto had been, "Fix it and move on!" I had always stressed to my employees, and especially my supervisors, "Never ignore a problem! If you try to sweep it under the rug, it will only raise its head later. And by then, it will cost ten times as much to address."

Of course, we wanted to try to do the job right the first time, but when a problem arose, I set out to solve it, without procrastination. Even if the decision or solution was not always the right one, it was good to take a proactive position. When the solution didn't work, or only partially solved the problem, I simply rethought things, keeping at the problem until I did solve it.

My ability to analyze things, think them through, come up with the best solution, and implement it, was ingrained in me. It was second nature for me to deal with problems swiftly and decisively.

• Making the Most of Past Experiences

They say that experience is the best teacher—and it seems we remember the difficult experiences most of all.

I can recall with painful clarity a great example of a situation that snowballed into a catastrophe, thanks to the decisions made by someone in my employ who failed to address a problem as it arose.

It happened while the company was growing at such a rate of speed that the growth had become overwhelming. The time had come to get someone to help me in the office. I already had one person on staff who would bid jobs. The individual I hired was a project manager. His job was to review, modify, change, and submit estimates to the clients, and manage the jobs we were in the process of performing. More often than not, a negotiation would follow, in which I would be involved.

What happened was this: The project manager was taking the losses from one job, and posting them to another job, and taking the costs from one job, and carrying them over to another job. His intention seemed to be to make the job-cost reports more attractive than their actual reality.

At the end of the day, I owed the bank a little better than $1,200,000.00—not that such an occurrence in and of itself was so unusual. But, something seemed fishy.

One day, I happened to stumble across a job-cost report. Reviewing it, a tiny item caught my eye—and sent off alarm bells inside me. I could see that something on the report had been moved or changed. It was a small detail, a one-line item that took money from one place, and put it in another. I began investigating, and even got my accountant involved.

The results of our investigation showed that this individual had moved in excess of $900,000.00 in costs, and carried them forward to other jobs, so as to make past jobs appear profitable when they were actually losing money!

I suspected the project manager of theft. My gut told me that he was authorizing additional costs to subcontractors—and having them do work on his house, or hire others to do work on his house—thus increasing our costs and losses, and creating the necessity to hide those numbers.

The problem was, he had so cleverly and carefully hidden, moved, and manipulated the data, nothing short of a full-blown forensic audit could have proven it. When all was said and done, I realized that resorting to a forensic audit and legal action wasn't worth the aggravation. So, I simply fired him.

Lesson one: Had the project manager come to me with whatever was on his mind when it first arose, and addressed it with me, that would have been the end of that. By choosing deception as a means of problem-solving, he created a huge mess, and ultimately found himself out of a job.

Lesson two—I can't accept something as the gospel truth simply because it is stated as such in some report. I must always look deeper, and refuse to be swayed by the superficial appearance of things. This is a lesson that would come in very handy later when reviewing case evidence.

• Understanding the Financial Aspects of Justice

It is important to understand that justice is not really quantifiable. The justice system cannot return to someone their limb, brain, ability to work, or whatever it was that was lost. And, it cannot bring people back from the dead.

So, civil cases *always* come down to money. Justice is dispensed through the finding of fault, and the awarding of money—the amount somebody determines a life, injury, or other loss, to be worth, financially.

In cases where someone has been injured, disabled, or even killed, one party to the case is seeking compensation for their loss—loss of life or limb, loss of quality of life, and so on. If the person is injured, the compensation they are seeking may not stop at mere payment of their medical bills. They may be taking a position of, "I am unable to work any longer, and I am only thirty-two years old! Had I not been injured, I could have worked for another thirty years, and earned X."

There are all sorts of experts that are hired to quantify value, and project the value of a working life span based upon occupation.

• Identifying the Intangibles

Just as with any other profession, an expert witness practice involves certain intangibles that go beyond the basic requirement of giving your opinions and conclusion on cases.

What are those intangibles?

For one thing, you will need an analytical mind—but merely being analytical isn't enough; you need analytical *dexterity*. Without it, you could easily be swayed to one side or the other by the emotional component of a case.

Obviously, people would not be involved in a dispute unless they had differing ideas as to who was in the right. Conflict, by its nature, tends to elicit high emotion. It is that emotional element that needs to be removed to the greatest degree possible, in order for settlement to occur. And, the way to remove the emotion of a case is by concentrating on the facts and the evidence.

That is what an expert is hired to do—evaluate the facts and evidence, weigh them against things like methods and means, standard industry practices, standards of care, and specific regulatory rules, and then form opinions and a conclusion. It is not an expert's job to become emotionally involved, and support or share the emotions or the position of the retaining counsel and/or their client.

With analytical dexterity, you evaluate the evidence, and express your opinions and conclusion truthfully, while at the same time making your report or testimony factual, believable, easily understandable to the lay person—*and convincing.*

Removing the emotional element is also the first thing any mediator or arbitrator will attempt to do in mediation, arbitration, or nonbinding arbitration. They know that they must set aside the emotional component so they can deal with the facts and the economics of the case at hand—and money is always a key factor in any civil proceeding.

As you will see, however, from the following example, emotion can impact a case even more than money:

Recently, I was working from home, and happened to turn on the TV. I began watching one of those court-TV shows. The dispute involved the attack upon one person's dog by another person's dog. The entire dispute boiled down to $161.00.

I said to my wife, "I cannot believe that two grown adults would go on court TV, or to any legal court for that matter, over a hundred and sixty-one dollars!"

The thing is, *it wasn't about the money!* It was about "I'm right, you're wrong, and you harmed me and/or my dog!"

Emotion is often at the heart of a dispute.

• Separating Fact from Fiction

Because the world of the expert witness is not one that many people inhabit, it carries with it a certain cachet, and experts command a certain level of respect. But, it is important to keep in mind that being an expert witness is not always like it is portrayed on TV!

When you're watching certain shows on TV, it's easy to get the impression that the judicial system provides a structured form of justice. And, it is true that the judicial system is structured *to a certain extent*. You have the rule of law, the (state and) Federal Rules of Civil Procedure, and the rules of court.

The law, itself, is subject to the discretion of the trier of fact. This goes against everything we want to believe. We would like to think that justice is black and white—either someone has been wronged or they haven't, and whoever is right prevails.

Reality is not that way. Only the truth is black and white. The law is a whole different story. A great example comes to mind. It was a case that was anything but black and white.

I personally had to sue one of my own subcontractors, whom I had hired to install a rather large asphalt parking lot as part of a commercial construction project. After the asphalt work was completed, the owner took core samples (as was common practice) to test for thickness, density, air voids, etc. The test results revealed deficiencies in all areas, but the overall compressed or compacted thickness of the asphalt was particularly deficient—by an inch to an inch-and-a-half.

I hired an independent testing agency to take core samples, and perform the necessary test to confirm or deny the owner's results. The test unequivocally confirmed the owner's conclusion that the thickness was deficient, and did not meet the specified requirements set forth on the drawings, and in the contract documents.

I immediately sent the subcontractor a notice to cure the deficiency—but the subcontractor refused, claiming that the thickness was within New Jersey Department of Transportation (DOT) standards.

A short time later, the owner notified me that a portion of the parking lot had failed. Once again, I sent the subcontractor a notice to cure. Again, he refused to repair the problem. Being responsible for my subcontractors, I promptly made arrangements to have the repairs made—but only on that part of the parking lot that had failed.

I was holding a 10% retainage—money withheld from the subcontractor's invoice, which was to be released upon completion of the job, once my company deemed their work to be acceptable, which we did not. In fact, their work was completely unacceptable!

The subcontractor took the position that I still owed him the unpaid balance for the job he did, and told me in very colorful language that he wasn't fixing anything. He clung to his position, *despite the overwhelming evidence and test reports.*

He left me no choice but to file a lawsuit. So, I sued the subcontractor for what he should have done but didn't, for what I had to do in order to fix the problem, and for what I might still have to fix because he refused to remedy the deficiency in the overall thickness of the asphalt.

During the initial stages of the legal action, my lawyer requested that I, as the principal of my company, be named as an expert witness. I hesitated because I felt that, being directly involved in the case, my testimony would be considered inherently biased by the jury or the judge.

I told my attorney that I felt that an independent asphalt expert should be retained. I also recommended that those whom I had hired to perform independent testing of the asphalt thickness and other asphalt properties, as well as the sub-grade soil analysis, be specifically named as expert witnesses.

The attorney claimed that it was unnecessary to name the other witnesses as expert witnesses, stating that they were *fact* witnesses, "Because they could testify as to what they do in the ordinary course of their business." Fact witnesses are permitted to testify under oath to a fact related to a particular matter in which they were directly involved, but not permitted to rely on hearsay (what others told them they said or did.)

I agreed to be named as an expert, and the attorney failed to name the other witnesses as experts—or intentionally chose not to, because he did not feel it was necessary. (Marvin Belli, Sr.'s quote seems especially applicable here: "Indeed, counsel who chooses to proceed without an expert may be flirting with malpractice.")

At trial, we called several fact witnesses. It bears repeating that fact witnesses differ from expert witnesses, who are allowed by law to testify on matters of hearsay. For example, as part of my testimony, I, as an expert witness, could say, "I interviewed John, and he told me that he saw the dump trucks arrive half full." Even though it is hearsay, I would be allowed to testify to its factual relevance.

A fact witness couldn't testify to that; it is hearsay. They could only testify to a fact they know to be true—something they witnessed or observed directly—or something they would do, or perform, in the ordinary course of their business.

Our attorney began by calling me to the witness stand, and asking me questions about the soil reports and the asphalt reports. The defense attorney quickly objected to my testimony, claiming that it was hearsay.

Our attorney—who had listed me as an expert witness—responded by saying, "Your Honor, Mr. Gulya is listed as an expert, and as such, can testify to such matters."

However, unbeknownst to me at the time, there had been a pretrial conference, overseen by a judge. During that conference, the judge set a date for all expert reports to be submitted to the court and opposing counsel. Despite the Court Order, our attorney did not ask me to provide an expert report, later stating to me that it was the defense's duty to ask me to provide a report.

Without being asked to prepare a report, I had not written or provided retaining counsel with one. I was abiding by a hard and fast rule that experts must follow: Never provide a written expert report unless it is specifically asked for and requested by the retaining counsel.

There are two good reasons for this. First, you could spend forty hours or more preparing a report that retaining counsel did not request—and therefore retaining counsel may not compensate you for it. Secondly, each state's Rules of Civil Procedure may vary. Some states, such as Florida, do not even require experts to provide a written report.

Because I had not submitted an expert report, the judge promptly sustained the defense counsel's objection. He ruled that I could not testify as an expert, because a report was not filed per the judge's Order in the pretrial conference.

As a direct result of this ruling, I was unable to testify to the soils report, or any other report I did not personally create. Since I had not met the criteria of an expert witness by submitting a written expert report, my testimony would have been considered hearsay. My testimony was thereby so limited as to be ineffective.

Part of the defense's position in the case was that the subsoil (the soil they laid the asphalt over) was substandard in some way.

So, we called the soil-testing company that was employed by the owner, and present on the job site every day. The owner had specifically hired and paid for the independent soil testing company themselves, to ensure that there was no collusion between the soil testing company and my firm.

The soil testing company was to test the soil compaction we provided, to assure the owner that we were performing our work according to the requirements set forth in the specifications—compaction of 95% or greater. They also tested the soil for moisture and other required properties.

The soils expert (named as a fact witness) called by our attorney was responsible for taking the data from the test his field technicians took at the jobsite, and putting it into a formal report. Now, he was not the *actual individual* at the job site; he has fifty technicians in his employ that go to various sites to perform the actual tests. Those technicians recorded the test data, which was reviewed by the fact witness, who put it in report format, and sent it to the owner and me.

To summarize, our fact witness was the guy who took the data, put it in report format for me to read, and stated, "Okay, test number one taken at Location 'A' showed 98% compaction. Test number two taken at Location 'B' showed 96%, and test three taken at Location 'C' showed 95%."

Our attorney began the direct examination of this witness. After the first few formality questions—such as his name, position, and who he worked for—our attorney asked the first question directly related to the test results report.

The defense counsel immediately objected, stating that the witness was not listed as an expert, and therefore could not testify to the accuracy of the report.

The judge asked the witness, "Sir, did you take each of the tests personally, or witness them being taken?"

The witness said, "No, Your Honor, I have technicians in my employ that do that."

The judge disallowed the fact witness's testimony entirely as hearsay, because he didn't actually take the test himself, nor did he witness the test being taken. Only an expert witness would have been allowed to testify to tests he did not personally perform, or witness directly.

Our attorney argued, "But this is what this man does in the ordinary course of his business! No one man can go down to the job site and take every single test. It is just not possible."

The judge stated, "I don't care. It's hearsay. He cannot testify to the accuracy of those tests, and therefore his testimony and report are not admissible. If you want these test results admitted, it's fine with me. Bring in every person that actually performed the tests."

"But, Your Honor," our attorney said, "that would be twenty different people, some of whom now live out of the country!"

To which he replied, "I don't care. That's your problem. Mr. X is not an expert, and cannot testify to the accuracy of the test. It is hearsay. "

Our next witness was to be the asphalt testing company representative. Like the soils witness, he also had technicians that took the tests. Our attorney didn't even bother to call him to testify, knowing that the same objection would be raised, and the same ruling would be imposed by the judge.

In the end, the testimony of two key witnesses, and their reports, were not admitted into evidence. Our case was in serious jeopardy.

The opposition rested their case—and why wouldn't they? The burden of proof was on the plaintiff to make their case, and we did not. The defense made the right decision, figuring there was no point in opening a can of worms that could potentially hurt them.

Ultimately, we lost the case to the tune of $94,000.00!

Our attorney admitted to me that he made a damaging error, by not asking me to provide an expert report, and not listing our other witnesses as experts. He also told me he would appeal the case, *pro bono*, due to his error. He was hopeful that the outcome might be reversed on appeal.

During the appellate proceedings, one of two judges on the panel looked at the defendant's attorney and said, in so many words, "Let me understand this. You have your own expert witness, and the plaintiff had an expert they had hired, both of which took core samples of the asphalt, and evaluated the results, to determine density, thickness, etc.

"Your own expert stated in his report that the asphalt was of insufficient thickness and outside New Jersey DOT's limits of acceptance, in the amount of one to one-and-a-half inches, according to the specified requirement. In addition your expert recommended that a one-and-one-half to two-inch overlay of the entire area would be the responsible solution and fix for this issue."

The defense said, in so many words, "That's correct, Your Honor."

The appellate judge continued, saying to the defendant, "You admit in your interrogatories that you didn't put down at least one-half to one-inch of asphalt thick enough. Yet, you want to be compensated as if you put down all the asphalt you were supposed to have installed?"

They said, "That's correct, Your Honor!"

The judge asked, "Why?"

"Well," they continued, "because we believe the company we were working for got paid for one hundred percent of the asphalt. Therefore, so should we!"

"But," the judge pointed out, "you and your own expert acknowledge that you did not install the full seven inches of asphalt, as specified. The trenching company has a responsibility to fix the deficiency—which has yet to be fixed because you won't fix it!

"So, even if they have been paid *every dollar owed them*, that is between them and the owner—who is not a party in this action. Does that mean you should be paid every dollar, when you failed to supply something to the required amount or thickness of material, and did not correct the deficiency?"

The judge took it one step further. "Let's say you didn't lay any asphalt at all. Would you still want all the money?"

The defense attorney was silent.

So, let's look at this situation. Did the civil judge in the initial lower-court trial make a whole bunch of questionable decisions and rulings based on law?

He certainly had the latitude to allow the fact witnesses to testify to what routinely occurs in the ordinary course of their business. And, he may have had the latitude to allow the test reports to be admitted into evidence, since these particular fact witnesses routinely submit such test results.

Was it unreasonable and irrational of the judge to expect that an employer of a major and respected testing company be required to bring in every worker who performed and gathered test data? Isn't that as ridiculous as expecting a physician to personally take every set of x-rays he orders for his patients?

A physician doesn't personally take a patient's x-rays; an x-ray technician does! You wouldn't be required to bring in the x-ray tech to testify as to the accuracy of the x-ray just because they took it. You would rely on the doctor who compiled the results of the x-ray.

In this case, the judges in the appellate court ultimately upheld and affirmed the lower court judge's decisions, specifically stating that the rulings of the lower court judge were sound and within the law.

They ignored the fact the defendant admitted that they did not install the proper thickness of asphalt material.

They ignored the fact that the defendant's own expert's report recognized, and acknowledged, a shortage of one to one-and-a-half inches of asphalt.

They ignored the fact that the defendant's own expert recommended that a one to one-and-a-half-inch overlay be added to the deficient thickness.

They even ignored the fact that the asphalt contractor should not be paid for something they did not provide, supply, or install!

Our attorney sent me an email with the bad news, saying "This is clearly not the result I was expecting. We will appeal to the appellate court for reconsideration."

The appellate court rejected our attorney's appeal for reconsideration. This was another severe blow to our case. As of this writing, the case is pending consideration before the State Supreme Court, and there has not yet been a decision as to whether they will agree to hear the case.

• **Following the Rules of Law**

This case—where the appellate judge ultimately carried the Hearsay Rule to the point of absurdity, and upheld the findings of the lower court—proves that, in a court of law, things are rarely black and white.

So, how could this case have gone so horribly wrong? At the end of the day, it all came down to one thing: The rules of law.

One—my attorney failed to list the witnesses as experts, and instead listed them as fact witnesses; and

Two—my attorney failed to inform me that I needed to submit an expert witness report according to the judge's pretrial conference Order.

The rules of law trumped the truth! The court turned a blind eye and a deaf ear to the truth—*despite the defense's admission of guilt!*

When you have someone who admits a wrong, but that admission is ignored, due to court procedure or rules, it makes you question the system.

So, I leave it to you, the reader, to decide…Was justice served in this case?

How about in the trial of Casey Anthony? Was justice served in that case? Both the American public and the media convicted her. The judicial system did not.

• Recognizing the Critical Role of Experts

There is another important lesson to take from the asphalt case: Expert witnesses are critically important, *precisely because* justice is rarely black and white, and the judicial system is inherently complex. This case was a great example of this fact.

The defense admitted the truth—that there was a shortfall in what they were supposed to provide. But, because there were only fact witnesses, and no expert witnesses, on our side of the case, *the truth could not be admitted into evidence!*

The witnesses—erroneously listed by our attorney as fact witnesses—could not testify as to the accuracy of various test result reports because the judge ruled that they were not experts.

Then there were the test results, themselves. There were three test-result reports in total—the soil report, the asphalt thickness/density/other properties report, and the defense's own asphalt expert's report, which acknowledged a shortage of material thickness, and recommended a fix.

None of those reports was admitted into evidence *because there were only fact witnesses listed, not expert witnesses.* And expert witnesses were the only ones who could have assured that admissibility.

• Identifying Your Niche

Excavation Safety (handwritten)

This case perfectly illustrates the critical role of expert witnesses in our judicial system—and it explains why there is such high demand for expert witnesses from every field imaginable. Even those who don't necessarily advertise themselves as experts get called to testify.

A good friend of mine, for example, is a dentist—and not a practicing expert witness. Nevertheless, he is asked from time to time to provide his expert witness testimony on a case. He always declines.

His reason is interesting. It is not that he is afraid of serving as an expert witness. And it is not that the idea doesn't appeal to him—it does. But, he says no because it does not make sense for him, financially. I know I have already stated that expert witnesses can command a good fee, and sometimes even an excellent one, *but only if they have a specialty or niche.*

As my dentist friend is fully aware, there are already a million general dentists out there, practicing as expert witnesses. The market is flooded. The same is true in the medical field. It stands to reason that, when there is more supply than demand, the bottom line is affected. The reality is, the less specialized an expert witness is, in terms of his experience and his field of expertise, the less they will be able to command, in terms of their fee.

This is why it is so important to find a niche. You will want to identify a niche, without making that niche too narrow, or limiting potential clients within your field of expertise.

Let's say you are, for example, an electrician who wants to establish himself as an expert. You may be one electrician amongst thousands. However, if you were to market yourself as an electrical expert specializing in audio-visual wiring concepts, you might find that you are part of a narrower field.

Once you've identified your niche, you are going to need to gear your marketing towards that specialty. And that marketing plan can't simply be a lawn sign, reading, "Joe Smith, Electrical Expert Specializing in Audio-Visual Wiring Concepts." If that is the extent of your marketing efforts, you are likely to attract only a handful of clients—attorneys who happen to have an electrical case, and happen to be driving by slowly enough to glimpse the sign, and note the phone number.

In a subsequent chapter, I will address various approaches to marketing your expert witness practice.

~ 3 ~
PREPARATION
Doing Your Due Diligence

"If you have an apple and I have an apple,
and we exchange apples,
then you and I will still each have one apple.
But, if you have an idea, and I have an idea,
and we exchange these ideas,
then each of us will have two ideas."
~ George Bernard Shaw

• **Managing Your Time**

★Time management is an important aspect of your expert witness business. As I mentioned in the introduction, an expert witness can face a highly unpredictable schedule.

So, what sort of a time commitment is required? Is it necessarily a full-time endeavor? Or, is it something you can pursue part-time?

As I set out to answer these questions for myself, I discovered that it is more common than not for an expert witness to have a full-time job or position within a company, or to be a principal within their

32

own company, doing expert work part-time. If you do not continue to work in your primary profession, you need to be mindful of the way that fact is disclosed to attorneys who may be deposing, or examining you, at trial.

It is the opposing attorney's first objective to chip away at your credibility, so one of the first questions they ask an expert during deposition or trial is, "Are you a full-time professional expert?" If the expert answers in the affirmative, their credibility is compromised.

In the event that you happen to be retired from your profession, you might want to answer that question as follows: "I am retired, and my expert witness work consumes twenty to thirty percent of my time." Your goal is to dispel the notion that you focus all of your attention on being an expert witness. Attorneys can take that and twist it to give the impression to the jury and/or judge that you are a "professional" expert witness, for sale to the highest bidder.

The amount of time an expert actually spends on a particular case can vary wildly, depending on many factors—how complex the case is going to be, and how voluminous the documents will be that require your review. One time, I was sent eighty—yes, eighty!—legal boxes of evidence on a case in which I was involved.

It can be tricky balancing your expert witness duties with the responsibilities you carry in the day to day operations of your business. The ease or difficulty of finding that balance will depend upon many things, including what is required of you in your full-time position. Depending upon your position, splitting your time between your job or profession and your expert witness practice may be easier or more difficult to manage.

In my case, as the owner of my company, I answer only to myself—and, of course, my clients. I have the discretion to decide which things need to get done at work, and which things I might be able to postpone in order to focus on a case. I never concern myself with putting off something at the office, because I work at home during evenings and weekends, whenever I need to catch up.

For example, I was retained by an attorney in Boston to opine on a case for a certain company. The attorney waited until the last moment, and had a very tight deadline to meet.

There I was, on vacation in Aruba, with family and friends, sitting under a palapa (straw tiki hut) on the beach, with my laptop. I had put all the evidence I needed to review on DVD or CD in PDF format, and I had all of it with me. So, while everyone else was sunning themselves and enjoying the water, I was reading evidence, taking notes, working on my out-line, and forming my report.

Everybody enjoyed teasing me, saying, "Oh, yeah, this is some vacation for you, Bill!"

To which I replied, "Yeah! I'm earning a good wage while working away on this beautiful beach. How about you? How much are you earning?" We all had a good laugh over that one.

In all seriousness, my family is very supportive and encouraging of my expert witness practice. They find the nature of the work I do to be fascinating, but, more importantly, they understand and appreciate the fact that I am contributing, by being of service to people in a meaningful way that impacts lives. Of course, they have always been proud of my success in business, but the expert witness life is quite different than pushing dirt from Point A to Point B.

• Setting a Fee For Your Services

How do you determine the right value for your services?

This is a sensitive and personal decision—and not as simple as it sounds.

As I began to research the subject, I discovered that expert's fees vary considerably, depending upon the line of work in which the expert has gained his experience. A brain surgeon working as an expert might charge $1,500.00 to $3,000.00 per hour. Someone who sweeps floors, on the other hand, might charge only $50.00 an hour.

I found a general rule of thumb. It makes sense to value your services based upon your particular expertise, and your years of experience in that field. As a starting point, you may want to charge a fee in the general range of what you would normally expect to be compensated for your time and expertise, in the usual course of doing business.

However, the value of an expert is not simply related to his usual hourly compensation. Being an expert witness requires a lot of work, and is a very stressful undertaking.

Let's continue with the example of the floor cleaner who charges $50.00 an hour to clean floors. There may be minimal stress involved in cleaning floors. On the other hand, being an expert witness is highly stressful. So, you can't really make a straight apples-to-apples comparison. You must also consider your experience as an expert.

I struggled with this issue for days. On the one hand, I had, at that time, over thirty-five years in site-work construction. On the other hand, I was just getting started as an expert witness. I did not want to price myself too low, realizing that an attorney might perceive a low fee as a sign that I was not a very good expert, and not very sought after.

Pricing yourself too low can also be perceived as a desperate attempt by an inexperienced expert to drum up business.

Attorneys know the average fee that experts in a given field will command. If your fee is too low, they might think something is wrong.

They generally feel that the higher the fee charged by an expert or consultant, the greater their ability, importance, or stature. There is a perceived value associated with price—and perception is reality. Take designer blue jeans costing hundreds of dollars, for example, versus everyday, bargain jeans. They are all blue jeans, but the designer brands carry a higher price tag.

At the same time, you don't want to set your fee *too high*, or attorneys might wonder why, and may shy away.

I decided to establish my initial value just above the average fee of other experts in various sectors of the construction industry. In that way, I was establishing an image as a good, sought-after expert, while still being competitive. On rare occasions related to economic conditions, or on especially large cases, I may alter my fee slightly.

It should be noted here that your value will rise as you garner more and more experience in your expert practice. People always want what they can't have, or what is seemingly hard to get.

As time goes by, you may be able to show that you are the author of a book, or have had articles published in law journals, or have testified effectively. All of these things raise your perceived value.

Listing high-profile case summaries on your website also bolsters the perception of your credibility and expertise, and shows that you are more sought after—which translates to the ability to command higher fees.

Of course, as with every profession, some experts are better than others within the same field of expertise. Different qualities and expertise are required to build a reputation as a great or renowned expert witness. Communication, writing, research, and other skills are involved. Some experts command much higher fees, because they are recognized in the legal community as renowned in their field.

There are many things that go into valuing yourself as an expert witness. Ultimately, the decision to charge a certain fee is purely strategic.

- **Valuing Your Services Strategically**

To use our example above, let's say that for twenty-five years you owned a floor cleaning service and, in that capacity, you cleaned office floors or school/gym floors and hallways. You would undoubtedly be pretty proficient after all those years, and an expert at cleaning many types of floor surfaces.

Now, you decide to become a floor cleaning expert witness.

One day, an attorney with a case where someone has slipped on a floor finds you and calls you, certain that you are the right expert for the case. He is ready to hire you, and asks you how much you charge. You tell him that you charge $195.00 an hour—although, for twenty-five years, you've been earning one-fifth of that hourly fee as a floor cleaner.

Even if the retaining attorney agrees to your fee, the opposing attorney is sure to question you, along the following lines: "So, Mr. Smith, nobody can deny that you are an expert at cleaning floors. And you're being paid quite well to be here today—in fact, you're being paid $195.00 an hour! That's a lot of money, Mr. Smith. For $195.00 an hour, wouldn't you say just about anything to support the retaining counsel's position?"

If you are getting $195.00 an hour—an amount *five times* more than you've ever earned before in your entire career—you need to be prepared to justify it.

Don't be afraid to say "Expert work is stressful and demanding."

Speak confidently and professionally. Talk about your continuing education, if applicable. Talk about

how this fee covers your overhead costs.
~~You are going to be grilled, so be prepared, or the opposing counsel will have an opening to discredit you.~~

• Using a Witness Coaching/Marketing/Training Firm

When building any business, there are two things that seem to tip the scales—marketing and performance. The more you market yourself in the proper places, the higher your likelihood to be recognized and retained.

At that point, it would come down to performance. If you perform well, the retaining attorney will remember that performance, and if he—or a colleague or friend—has another case that involves your particular expertise, he will keep you in mind.

I began to research the best way to go about setting up and marketing my practice. If I was going to do something, I wanted to do it right the first time, remembering the words of my grandfather, "Measure twice, cut once!"

I carefully researched marketing firms. While researching online, I came across many services that presented themselves as expert witness services and yet did not seem to have the faintest idea what an expert actually does. Others were too large and expensive. Then, I found a firm called Expert Communications, which specializes in expert witness marketing, coaching, and training (www.expertcommunications.com).

At a glance, I could tell that this firm seemed to offer exactly what I was looking for—they specialize in expert witness practices.

I placed a call and spoke to the owner, Rosalie Hamilton. She is considered "the expert's expert," and is a truly lovely lady. She works as a marketing consultant, dealing exclusively with expert witness practices. She guides experts in establishing and building their practices, and is a one-stop knowledge and guidance center.

She came across in a manner that was straightforward and honest, and she obviously had my best interests at heart. She was someone I felt I could rely on to keep me on the right path, in terms of establishing and growing my practice.

It seemed like I had a thousand questions for Rosalie, but she had even more questions for me. She has very high standards, in terms of who she accepts as a client, and she wanted to be sure I met those high standards before we reached any agreement.

She interviewed me in great depth, to get a good understanding of me and my experience and expertise. The initial interview is free of charge, and at the end of it, she makes a decision as to whether or not she is interested in taking on the expert witness as a client.

Rosalie accepted me as a client, and within a week of our first conversation, she determined what she needed as a retainer, and she went to work on my behalf.

She took me by the hand and walked me through getting my expert witness practice up and running—the right way, the first time. She tailored her suggestions to my particular situation.

Could I have done everything myself? Sure. I could have built my own website, and researched expert witness directories and referral agencies.

For me, using a firm like Rosalie's was a twofold decision. First, I asked myself—can I afford this amount of money, and do I want to invest it in this way? And, secondly, I had to ask myself—if I choose to do everything myself, can I be sure that I am going about it in the right way, that my website meets the highest possible standards, and that I am reaching the right audience?

In my estimation, it was far better to know that everything was being set up professionally and correctly the first time. Sure, it cost more money, but most good things do. I was able to afford it, and there was no question in my mind that it was the way to go.

Someone in a different situation, who had time to burn at the end of the workday, might prefer to spend their evenings online, researching the various available resources.

For me, time is money, and I don't believe I would have been saving either one by blindly wandering around in the dark, trying to find the resources I needed to get my practice off the ground. In my case, it was an easy decision.

In the end, between Rosalie Hamilton's fees and the other associated costs of getting the practice started, including the website creation, and listing my services with referral agencies and directories (each of which might cost $500.00 or so, annually), I spent in the neighborhood of $20,000.00 to $25,000.00.

I feel that the money spent was well invested.

• Designing Your Website

Our first order of business? A website. I had to build it before they would come.

It is a widely shared opinion that a *professionally designed* website is one of the most important advertising and marketing tools any business can have. Generally speaking, an online search is going to be the first action taken by most attorneys when looking to hire an expert witness.

Many attorneys may not even be aware that expert witness directories and referral agencies exist, or may prefer not to use those that charge them a fee.

Rosalie referred me to a web designer, provided consultation as the website came together, and reviewed it when it was complete. It wasn't long before, in collaboration, we had created a professionally designed and built website, CV, and marketing plan.

• Creating your Curriculum Vitae (CV)

You should create a professional looking CV and post it on your website. You should also make sure you have it as a Word document or PDF, which you can easily email to attorneys or print as necessary.

A brief but well prepared CV will give attorneys basic information about you and your expertise, and entice them to call and interview you—which is exactly what you want. During the interview, the attorney will ask questions to gain a more in-depth sense of your qualifications, demeanor, personality, and expertise.

When writing your CV, there are two schools of thought: one—include as much information as you can; and, two—include only the most essential information.

I subscribe to the second approach. I believe that it is best to prepare a CV that is professional, neat, and includes only enough information to give an attorney a sense of your qualifications, background, and education. It should also include a photograph of you, so that an attorney can get a sense of your professional appearance.

Be sure to include in your CV the following:

A clear definition of your field(s) of expertise and a brief outline of your background in that field—where you have worked, what positions you have held, and for what length of time;

Your education and other professional training;

A listing of licenses, certifications (OSHA, for example), and any special training (safety training, for example) you might have received; and

A listing of any published articles or books you have to your credit.

Naturally, your contact information should be prominently displayed, and should include office phone and fax numbers, as well as your cell phone number and email address.

Do not fill up your CV with details of your experience or a list of cases. These things should be displayed in a separate area of your website.

(To see an example, the reader may peruse my CV at my website: www.siteworkexpert.com.)

• Listing Yourself with Referral Services and Expert Directories

Once I had my professionally designed website and CV, the next step was to be listed with various expert referral services and online directories. Rosalie helped me determine which expert witness directories I should be listed in, which expert referral services I should use, where I should advertise, and where I should not.

She listed me with several well-known and well-respected expert referral services and directories, including Forensis Group, TASA, JurisPro, HG Experts, and others. These services differ in the way they charge experts. Some charge you an annual fee to be listed in their database, and some add a fee on top of your fee, on any cases where you have been hired through their service.

• Understanding the Benefits of Publishing Articles

The next best thing to a professionally designed and well-functioning website is to be published.

While most experts will agree that they may only get a certain amount of work from expert referral agencies and directories, those very same referral agencies, and online directories can be a great resource for publishing articles. Many of them publish the articles of their member experts. I have found that the annual membership fee I pay to belong is worth the opportunity it affords me to post my articles.

I have also published articles in law journals and publications that are widely read by attorneys—my target audience. Law journals, like other print publications, have editorial calendars that set forth the various themes or segments of law upon which they might be focusing at any particular time. One month, they might be focusing on real estate law, the next month on business law, and the month after that on construction law. If I keep an eye on their editorial calendar, I can match my expertise with their editorial theme.

Some of my articles are directed at attorneys, and some at expert witnesses. The ones directed at other experts are for placement on websites of referral agencies and online directories.

The things I write for other experts are also read by attorneys, when they are visiting those websites looking for experts, or visiting my own website, where my articles are posted.

How do I know? Because I have been hired by attorneys who have visited those websites and read an article I've written. While an attorney may not care one way or another about *what* one expert has to say to another, they can't help but notice *the way it is said.* In a business where my ability to get hired is dependent upon my ability to communicate well, I value any opportunity that allows me to show my communication skills.

When attorneys read articles published by experts, they are inclined to think, *This guy knows what he is talking about.*

In the expert witness business, as in all other industries, perception is reality! That is true in every aspect of the business. Attorneys, jurors, and judges will all be taking note of the language in your report, your demeanor, your appearance, everything.

If they perceive you to be truthful, professional, and believable, they are going to believe you over someone else. It is as simple as that.

~ 4 ~

PRESENTATION
Marketing Your Services

"Destiny is no matter of chance.
It is a matter of choice.
It is not a thing to be waited for;
It is a thing to be achieved."
~ William Jennings Bryan

- **Subtlety and Decorum**

There are two words you must always keep in mind when developing any sort of marketing presentation—subtlety and decorum. All content, regardless of where it appears, should have the ring of subtlety and decorum to it.

Any marketing content or approach that smacks of salesmanship is going to defeat your entire purpose. In fact, it would be better to do no marketing and leave it up to chance than it would be to do a hard-sell type of marketing campaign.

Even the word marketing, itself, is tricky. What you actually want to do is *inform*. The goal should always be to let attorneys know of your existence, and give

47

them a brief synopsis of your expertise and experience as an expert witness. Anything more than that, and you will be shooting yourself in the foot.

➤ Your very ability to be taken seriously as an expert depends upon subtlety and decorum. It needs to come through in everything you do, wear, write, and say—and especially in your marketing pieces.

• Marketing via Email

I remember thinking, *Email blasts! What a perfect way to reach hundreds, if not thousands, of attorneys quickly.*

There was only one downside, and it was a big one: Any email addresses you use must be obtained thru opt-in permission, or you could be accused of spamming.

As someone deeply involved with the legal profession, I needed to be very careful that I was not violating spam laws. Along with whatever trouble might await me, I could also permanently damage my reputation. The reputable email marketing companies are certified, use double and triple opt-in listings, have removal links available at the bottom of all emails, and do everything in accordance with the law.

Since the only attorney email addresses I had were the ones I used in my construction business, I decided that it made sense to invest in an opt-in list of attorney email addresses. It wasn't cheap but, after all, I was making an investment in my new practice, so I approved the cost.

I used a marketing professional to develop the content, with subtlety, decorum, and professionalism in mind. Then, my website designer put together the HTML code for the email blast, to ensure that the email I sent out would be high-end and compatible with most browsers.

I was excited at the prospect of how many attorneys I might reach—until the results of the email blast arrived. The data showing how many recipients actually opened the email were well below the statistical averages, and quite disappointing.

In my view, it was a failure. Then I recalled something I had read—*it only takes one case to potentially recover your marketing investment.* I still held out hope.

Not a single case ever came of that email blast. On the other hand, my message was in the hands of the one hundred attorneys who did actually open and read the email. And who knows? One day they may need my services and think to themselves, *Wait a minute! I remember getting an email from a guy who may be just the kind of expert I am looking for!"*

With that in mind, I have since commissioned other email blasts, expanding the area to cover the entire United States. My focus was no longer centered on how many opened the email, but on the fact that the email blast gave me exposure to ten thousand attorneys and law firms that may need my services in the future.

Initially, I had been certain that sending out between fifty thousand and a hundred thousands emails with a clear, distinct, and professionally designed message would be instantly gratifying and rewarding. The opposite turned out to be true. If it was ever to be a gratifying or rewarding experience, it would be a matter of having the right email hit the right person at the ideal moment. Such a thing is completely beyond my control.

I took several things away from this experience:

I needed to be certain that I always performed email blasts with legally obtained opt-in email addresses from reputable firms; I shouldn't get caught up in the statistics; and I should approach this method of promotion with the sole purpose of potential exposure down the road.

• Marketing via Direct Mailing

Between email marketing and direct marketing, it is hard to name the superior marketing approach. They are two different mediums that ultimately accomplish the same goal. And the success of either depends upon timing and the need of the recipient.

Between the two, I personally prefer direct mailing. Following are my reasons why.

At the end of each email marketing campaign, I receive from the email marketing company a report, listing the number of people who did and did not open the email, as well as the number that bounced back, and therefore were not delivered. With an email blast, if I sent out fifty thousand and 15% opened it, I would consider myself lucky.

That same sort of statistical information is unavailable with a direct marketing campaign. I have no way of knowing whether the recipients looked at, and perhaps saved, the mailer, or tossed it right into the garbage. There are those mailers perceived as junk that get thrown away immediately, and there are those that get sorted into a pile for the recipient to revisit at a later date.

While the email medium provides a statistical analysis detailing the outcome of the campaign, and the direct marketing campaign does not, the reality is that with either, it is about exposure, exposure, exposure. You send something out, and maybe it sticks and maybe it doesn't. At least with direct mailing, you have a tangible product, something that the recipients can hold in their hands and hopefully say to themselves, "Well, this looks good!"

In my estimation, even the best looking email, complete with graphics, cannot compete with a mailer that is eye-catching, colorful, well-designed and beautifully printed, and full of interesting content. There is something about the tangible mailer that causes the recipient to pay more attention.

Ultimately, I feel that a direct-marketing mailer is more effective than email, which has become so ubiquitous, automatic, and sterile, few people even pay attention to it anymore. And, with the sophistication of spam and junk filters, many promotion emails are never seen, regardless of the number of times they are sent.

Sure, it takes time to compose the advertising, create the artwork, label and send the mailers. But, developing a regular direct-marketing plan targeted to your audience can pay huge dividends.

• Preparing Your Direct Mailer

I personally prefer the postcard format. I use an oversized, simple card with a couple of nice looking graphics related to the judicial system, and some graphics showing heavy equipment used in the construction business.

On one side of the card is language stating that each client's case is important, and an experienced expert can make a difference in the outcome. I also include a testimonial quote or two. On the right side, I list my name, phone number, and some details related to my expertise. The opposite side contains the bulk mailing label.

The key to using direct mailing as a means of marketing is to be consistent and constant. With each mailing, the layout and format remain constant. The only thing that changes is the testimonial section of the postcard—and the color. One time I might use blue; another time, I might use bronze, gold, or green.

Recognition is the key. After the recipient has received the mailer two or three times, they will come to recognize and remember the sender. Even if the mailer goes directly into the circular file, the person tossing it is likely to remember who sent it.

The consistency part of the equation relates to the intervals at which the mailer is sent. The length of the interval is not as important as remaining consistent— although sending a mailer at three-week intervals is probably a bit too frequent, and sending out annual mailers is too infrequent.

For me, I use a three-month interval. I send out about fifteen thousand mailers at a time, in bunches of two thousand. The first two thousand get mailed. Then, I wait two weeks and send out two thousand more, and so on. This way, the recipients that received it at the beginning on the first mailing will be the same ones that receive it at the beginning of subsequent mailings.

• Informing—Not Advertising

It bears repeating—the one thing my mailers *never* do is give the impression I am an ambulance chaser, so to speak, promising a special deal for this week only, or twenty-five-percent off my usual rate if the recipient responds within the next three days.

I am careful that my mailers never come across as solicitations or advertisements. They are more like oversized business cards I would hand to attorneys I encountered in person. The message is along the lines of, "I am here if I can be of service to you. Here are my particulars and my contact information."

Truly, that is my only goal—to let attorneys know that I am here, and available, in the event they need my services. I am not running a blue-plate special, or letting them know about the monthly blowout sale.

There is a very important reason—aside from the obvious—that my mailers never contain any advertising stunts. When I am giving my oral testimony, one of the questions I am asked by attorneys is, "Do you advertise your services?" When I answer in the affirmative, I am then asked, "So, isn't your opinion in fact for sale?"

"No, sir," I always reply, "I am not paid for my opinion; I am compensated for my time." My mailer needs to always give that same impression.

Currently, my mailing list contains eleven thousand attorneys or law firms. It is entirely possible that one day, I will see one of those attorneys sitting opposite of me in a deposition or trial setting. Given that attorneys always do their due diligence, they could very well have knowledge of me—and my mailer—before I ever walk into that conference room for deposition or that courtroom for trial.

They will always be looking to attack my credibility, and the last thing I want is to give them something they can use against me.

• Being Wary of What You Post Online

Networking websites such as Linkedin www. linkedin. com can provide information, good and bad. They can provide your practice with exposure, but experts need to beware! Anything posted on such a site is fair game and can be used by attorneys to discredit you.

Experts in almost any field occasionally need assistance in determining the best method and means to present a point, or support it in a report. The internet is a fabulous source of information—with blogs, Twitter, Facebook, and specialty discussion boards on almost any subject, or field of expertise you can imagine.

However, if you want to keep something private, don't post it on the internet—*or the entire world will have access to it!*

As an expert, virtually everything you write or post becomes a discoverable record, available to anyone with the vigor and persistence to find it. And that is the inherent problem experts face in seeking the opinions or advice of other experts on a discussion board or blog—your communications are all discoverable! When an expert seeks advice in these types of forums, it is available to almost anyone, including, of course, the opposing counsel in the case the expert is working on.

Recently, I followed a discussion, wherein an expert was seeking opinions on how to best present to a jury a complex testing method set forth in his report. Several experts responded to his query, each offering his or her advice and opinion. However, as the discussion progressed, it became a debate over the types of testing methods, and the accuracy of each, the point of the original question (how to best present and explain the expert's findings) quickly getting lost.

The experts ignored the fact that one of the possible ramifications of publicizing their opinions on the testing methods was that such opinions could potentially be used against them in future cases.

It is a good policy to keep any questions and queries to other experts private.

You can call experts you know and have private phone conversations with them. Or, you can look up experts on the internet, and call them. You will find that most are willing to extend professional courtesy to you, by sharing their experience on the question at hand.

Do not use discussion boards, email, or any other online communication. It is all discoverable—and overzealous attorneys will look to discredit experts for even the most innocent discussions. They will take a discussion out of context, and twist it around, in an attempt to score a few unearned, unjust points with the jury.

Experts need to be aware of this, and be prepared to address and justify any exchanges, dialogues, or discourse on the matter. It is also important to note that, from time to time, you will be retained to opine on a case where you are instructed that you must not, under any circumstances, discuss the case with anyone other than your staff.

• Encouraging Word-of-Mouth Referrals

Most professionals know others within their work community, and occasionally see each other at conferences, outings, or other industry-wide events. Attorneys are no different.

The best advertising you could ever have is one attorney talking to another, saying, "I had this site-work project where a guy was tragically killed in a terrible construction accident, and I'll tell you, I hired this expert, and he did a great job for me!"

You can't buy that kind of advertising. What you can do is encourage good word-of-mouth by striving to be the best expert witness you can be, every single time you are retained.

No amount of emailing, direct mailing, or law journal advertising can touch word-of-mouth referrals in terms of their value to your business.

Word of mouth can also be the *worst* type of advertising if you have not been doing a good job. Word gets around. You can't take your expert duties lightly; you need to be constantly diligent. I can't repeat it enough—the work you do is of critical importance to the clients represented by the attorney who retained you. It can affect their entire lives.

It is a responsibility worthy of your very best effort—and it is of the utmost importance that you do the best possible job, with professionalism and integrity. Ultimately, your report and your testimony are your products; often, the outcome of the entire case may rest upon them. Without exception, they are what your reputation, good or bad, will be built upon.

Of course, from time to time, every expert will encounter some sort of difficulty with an attorney, and you may worry that your reputation is on the line.

I had just such a situation one time. It was a case that involved a paving contractor who was resurfacing a parking garage deck. A lady allegedly tripped, fell, and was injured in what is called an asphalt divot—a freshly laid asphalt area with a depression in it, caused by the weight of a car turning its wheels in the asphalt before it was completely hardened. (A divot is not so much a hole as a sunken impression.)

The lady parked her car, got out, and was walking to the entrance of a building when she allegedly tripped and fell in one of these asphalt divots. The depression was not more than an inch or so in depth, but enough to catch her heel.

The retaining attorney, who was rather aggressive with me from the very beginning, wanted me to test the asphalt material.

I told him in no uncertain terms that I felt that testing of the asphalt was unnecessary, and would serve no particular purpose, due to the fact that the evidence from the asphalt manufacturer clearly indicated that their asphalt mix design for that period of time was tested, and found to be within the state standards.

Regardless, the attorney felt that it was a bad mix that may have contained too much liquid, asphalt, or sand. He felt strongly about that because of the strong feelings of his client—the general contractor, who had hired the subcontractor who had laid the asphalt. His client's position was that he was not at fault—there was a problem with the asphalt mix.

Well, the evidence did not bear out the claim that the asphalt mix was bad.

I contacted the asphalt manufacturer, who was able to discuss the case with me, as they were not named as a party to the suit. They explained to me that they had already been contacted and provided the batch test results, which showed no problem.

I told the attorney that there was nothing wrong with the asphalt mix, and said that if he was under the impression that I could say that there was something wrong with it when I had no evidence to prove that claim, he was sorely mistaken.

He said, "I am not asking you to say something you can't prove. I'm asking you to test the asphalt!"

I said, "Okay, if you really want the asphalt tested, fine. But understand this—testing the asphalt becomes a double-edged sword. The tests will either show that the mix is good, and up to spec, or, they will show that it's not. My best information indicates that it's going to show that it's a good mix, because that's what the evidence already tells me. Once I do this test, I will have to acknowledge, when asked, that I performed this test—and I will have to reveal what the results showed."

He said, "No, you do not have to! You can bury it in your file."

To which I replied, "Oh, no, I can't! And I won't!"

Three days later, I received a letter stating that my services were no longer required by the attorney.

I stood by my ethics. The fact that the attorney chose to replace me was fine with me. I was not going to lie or withhold information.

I could just see the case going to deposition or trial, and somebody getting wind of the fact that I had performed the asphalt tests—and excluded the results from my report!

Naturally, they would question me as to why. Even if I said that the new test results were irrelevant, because there was supporting evidence already showing that the mix was good, the opposing attorney could say, "You deliberately withheld test results, good or bad, from your report, did you not?"

I would have no choice but to admit to having done so—and no one would believe another word I said in my report. My credibility would have been tarnished, if not shattered.

That was the first, and last, time I ever received a letter stating that my services were no longer required.

Was I concerned that this attorney might bad-mouth me, and become a source of "bad advertising" for me?

Yes, very! And, at that time, I did not yet have enough experience with attorneys to know any better than to be concerned.

I turned for guidance to the one person I was sure could help me—Rosalie Hamilton. Given that she deals with experts and their issues and problems every day, I knew she would have some wisdom to share with me.

When I got her on the phone, I explained, "Rosalie, I think I have a problem here…"

She told me, in so many words, that if the attorney wanted to speak badly of me, it would only reflect poorly on him. She asked me, "What would he tell his fellow attorneys—the ones you are concerned might hear something about you and decide not to hire you? That he had tried, unsuccessfully, to manipulate the opinion of a witness?"

"So," Rosalie concluded, "you need not concern yourself in the least about this. There is no way that attorney is going to run around town telling people you are a bad expert because you stood up for what is ethically correct! He was in the wrong here! He did the unethical thing by even asking you to withhold the results of a test you would have performed!"

Asking me to commit an unethical act was unethical of the attorney. My refusal to do so was not unethical.

I have had other experiences with difficult attorneys where there was nothing unethical asked of me, or even implied. I was not being expected to do anything beyond analyzing the facts and opining truthfully. The attorneys were just very difficult people.

The bottom line for me in those cases? The attorney is my client and, whenever possible, I must find a way to deal with their particular personality quirks. It is my job to serve my client to my best ability.

What if an attorney wanted to dismiss, fire, or replace me for reasons that seemed arbitrary and were unrelated to ethics, honesty, or ability?

My response would be, "Fine. So be it." I would be unconcerned. It is a fact of life that not everyone—attorneys or otherwise—is going to like me. If an attorney wanted to bad-mouth me, there would not be much that I could do about it.

If they did not have grounds to be speaking badly of me, they would look foolish. If they did have grounds, all I could, and would do, is apologize for whatever I had done to rub them the wrong way.

The best defense I have? To continually endeavor to do my best. That way, I never provide any attorney with a basis to give me less than a stellar reference.

~ 5 ~
BEGINNINGS
Getting Your Practice Going

*"Honesty is the first chapter
in the book of wisdom."*
~ Thomas Jefferson

• **Covering Your Bases**

What about errors-and-omissions or malpractice insurance? Was that something I was going to need to purchase?

I quickly discovered it wasn't necessary. The best way to cover my bases was by telling the truth, the whole truth, and nothing but the truth, based on the evidence. And, to always take great care to follow the Rules of Civil Procedure, as dictated by state or federal court.

Could somebody potentially sue me for my opinions, conclusion, or testimony, even though I was telling the truth? The very fact that I was offering my *opinions* and conclusion was built-in protection. The experts retained by the opposition have their opinions, as well, and they could differ, to the point of being completely opposite of mine.

The opposition's expert and I would be basing our opinions and conclusions upon our interpretation of the facts as we understood them, but, at the end of the day, it would still be only our opinions. This was a good reason to steer clear of absolutes, unless someone asked me something as irrefutable as my gender or date of birth, for example.

As long as I always tell the truth, there are no circumstances I am aware of that could result in a lawsuit being brought against me by a retaining attorney. Having said that, there is no precaution I can take that will preclude any person from availing themselves of their constitutional right to bring a lawsuit against me.

Do I worry about attorneys deciding they have an issue with me? No.

As for the retaining attorney, my agreement with them always includes language to the effect that the retaining attorney had the opportunity, prior to hiring me, to investigate my background and qualifications. I use the following language: *Client has had the opportunity to investigate and verify Consultant's credentials, and agrees that Consultant is qualified to perform the services described in this contract.*

If they later say that I harmed their case, by virtue of the fact that my background or qualifications did not fit the case for which they retained me, I am not responsible. They had the opportunity to check me out in advance, and made their decision to retain me or not accordingly.

The reason I include such language is to protect myself from what is known as a Daubert Challenge— a situation in which the opposing counsel requests a hearing before a judge for the purposes of challenging the validity and admissibility of an expert's testimony. This is one of the biggest concerns of experts—that their qualifications or testimony will be challenged.

In a Daubert hearing, the expert is required to demonstrate that his methods and reasoning are scientifically valid, and can be applied to the facts of the case.

Here is the way I see this: I am dealing with sworn testimony and documented evidence acquired through the legal system's discovery process, and sworn to under oath, penalties of perjury, and other penalties of law.

As long as I stick to the truth, I don't need to concern myself with potentially adverse consequences.

- **Utilizing Research Assistants**

Another question came up: Do I need to hire a research assistant?

Not necessarily. Then again, I might end up with a heavy case load, and having the benefit of some assistance would be a good thing. I also could see the value of having someone to bounce ideas around with, offer perspectives I might not have yet considered, and be an extra set of eyes.

Of course, at the end of the day, there are things I would never delegate—the actual writing of the report, for example. And, regardless of what a research assistant might come up with, it is my duty and responsibility to review their research, double-check it, and make sure it is applicable to the circumstances of the case.

• **Expanding Your Knowledge Base**

I wanted to arm myself with as much information as I could get my hands on.

I bought and read virtually every book I could find on the subject of being an expert witness. After reading one or two of them, I realized how much there was to learn regarding procedure, reports, evidence, marketing, record keeping, etc. I studied relentlessly, and made a commitment to myself to continually educate and update myself.

I did everything humanly possible to learn about the expert witness life—but I still didn't feel like it was sufficient. My testimony could affect the outcome of the cases on which I would be hired to opine, and people's lives hung in the balance. I owed it to myself, and more importantly, to my clients, to be the very best I could be.

The deep desire to further my education had always been there—especially as it related to court cases in which my construction company would be involved from time to time. But, I had been so busy running the company, I never found time to drop everything and go attend a university someplace.

Every time I would find myself involved in litigation for my own company, regardless of the nature of the case, I was reminded of my desire to pursue higher education. This reminder came in the form of a standard question always posed by the attorneys deposing me: "What is your level of education?"

I always answered with the response, "High school, with some college." I was never able to say, "I have a degree in X from XYZ institution."

The minute my answer came out of my mouth, everything changed. It wasn't just the next words spoken by the attorney; it was the expression on their face that said, "Oh…I see…so you're not a college-educated individual."

From that moment on, there would be a subtle shift in their demeanor towards me. I always felt that, in some unspoken way, they saw me as someone of a lower caliber, someone not quite as capable as a degreed individual.

I don't hold that belief, personally. But, sometimes, it seems that the rest of the world shares the perception that if you're a high school graduate, with little or no college under your belt, you are not quite as competent as a college graduate. The fact that someone has years of experience in a certain field seems to make little impression on people of that mindset.

Whenever I was put in the position of having to answer the education question in a deposition, I always felt uncomfortable—primarily because I disagreed with the assumptions made about me following my answer.

What could I do? I had to live with that perception from people. Meanwhile, the passion to rectify the situation, and enter college, continued to burn inside of me.

Ultimately, the passage of time, and the advent of online education, allowed me the opportunity to achieve my goal. While such technology has existed for years, it really came into its own relatively recently, and is now widely recognized and accepted as a structured, certified, approved alternative to attending classes in person. Today, there are many online colleges, including Kaplan, Phoenix, Ashford, and others.

In 2004, I enrolled in an online program offered through the University of North Carolina at Wilmington. I received my degree in Mediation and Alternative Dispute Resolution.

Just as attorneys continually stay involved with "Continuing Education of the Bar" coursework throughout their career, I understand the importance of doing the same. So, I recently enrolled in online coursework through Ashford University Online, where I am currently seeking my B.A. degree in communications.

In selecting my major, I chose one that would best support the kinds of tasks I am required to perform as an expert witness. The communications degree was a perfect fit, as it was heavily weighted in writing of all forms, but was geared more towards technical and analytical writing.

Thanks to my communications courses, I am better able to work with language, which shows in the formatting, vocabulary, and overall quality of my reports. I currently hold a 3.78 GPA, and I have made the dean's list and the *cum laude* list every semester.

Did I have to further my education in order to become successful as an expert witness? No, but because I chose to do so, I have often had attorneys tell me, "Your reports are some of the best I have seen." Or, "Your report was excellent." Or, "Your report was instrumental in settling this case."

Do you need a degree in order to pursue a career as an expert witness?

Only if the field in which you are claiming experience and expertise requires higher education of some sort. If one were, for example, a neurobiologist by profession, and after extensive years of working in their field, decided to establish an expert witness practice, they would need to have completed whatever level of education appropriate for, and expected of, a practicing neurobiologist.

If, on the other hand, someone was a thirty-year electrician, who did not claim to be an electrical engineer with any sort of advanced degree, then a college education would not necessarily be required.

Do I still think a degree would enhance their qualifications and credibility? Absolutely. I also believe that furthering their education would enable them to better serve their clients.

What I don't believe is that the world should view those without advanced degrees as somehow inferior. That said, the world is the way it is, and I cannot change it. So, sometimes it is better to just roll with it.

- **Staying Up to Speed on Knowledge Specific to Your Field**

Although you don't necessarily need a degree, as explained above, you are presenting yourself as an expert in your field of expertise. So, it is critical that before you hang out your shingle, and declare yourself open for business, you make sure you are up to speed with any specialized knowledge that may pertain to your industry.

In my field, for example, it is imperative that we know what the OSHA standards and regulations state, and when and how to apply them. We also need to understand OSHA citations that are issued, and why.

I am very familiar with OSHA regulations and standards. Surprisingly, there are thousands of contractors who are not. They have no idea what is required of them. So, they are often caught off guard when OSHA inspectors perform surprise inspections, of a job site. That does not happen very often, considering the fact that, in any given week, there are thousands of job sites, large and small, across the country. OHSA inspectors couldn't possibly inspect them all.

If, however, there is a serious injury or death on a job site, you can be sure that OSHA is right there, investigating the accident.

Just as I often need to use my knowledge of OSHA regulations, you also need to have up-to-date and comprehensive knowledge of your field of expertise.

• **Preparing for Interaction with Attorneys**

Throughout the years of running my company, legal conflicts would occasionally arise, and I ended up with a certain amount of experience in the legal system. That didn't mean I had a realistic perspective on attorneys.

Of course, like everyone else who lives in America, I had heard all the generalizations, jokes, and derisive comments made at the expense of lawyers. And, I have to admit, I had my own reservations about attorneys. To some extent, my ambivalence arose from frustrating interactions with our company attorney.

As I said, when I was young, I worked for my father during summer vacations—me, and half the Edison, N.J. Fire Dept., who worked for my father to pick up some side money!

Anyway, during those summers, I watched a guy named Fred, whom my father had known for years, go through college and law school, and eventually become, for all practical purposes, our company attorney.

No matter what sort of problem arose that required Fred's attention, it seemed he always had the same thing to say to me: "Listen, Bill, you have to keep better records! Document everything!"

But, it didn't seem to make any difference how thoroughly I prepared our files and records during the course of a project we were working on. If it ended up in litigation, Fred would tell me that we didn't have sufficient documentation, or our records weren't detailed enough.

At the time, I believed I was giving Fred everything he asked me for, and yet he was impossible to satisfy in this regard.

It was only after I penetrated the legal community to the degree required for an expert witness to function, that I began to develop a full appreciation of the amount of hard work that goes into practicing law. That's when I realized that Fred, and other lawyers with whom I had interacted as the principal of my company, had good reason for telling me I needed to *triple-document everything*.

They said that because it was true! You can never do enough, document things well enough, or be well enough prepared. The legal system thrives on voluminous documentation. And, no matter how much documentation you have, you *still* don't necessarily win your case. These are the kinds of things that make the practice of law so involved, and so difficult for attorneys.

I now have a better understanding of attorneys, and a genuine respect for their hard work.

• Interviewing with Attorneys

The attorneys retaining me are located all over the country.

I am able to work for attorneys nationwide because, most of the time, attorneys do not require an in-person meeting before retaining you. There may be several factors behind this, but the main reason is that they have already done their due diligence. They have researched your background, and possibly even called some of your attorney references before they ever initiated the first contact with you.

At that point, they are fairly comfortable with your qualifications. The way you present yourself in person comes through later. There is a lot of road to travel between the time you are retained, and the time you go to deposition or trial, where you would need to present well.

For these reasons, attorney interviews are usually handled over the phone, or by Skype.

Keep in mind, the phone interview is really a job interview. Attorneys will often know some buzzwords related to your field of expertise, and will be listening for the expert to use those words as the phone interview moves forward.

An attorney interviewing you will *always* have done enough research on their end to know things that are not common knowledge to the lay person. Now they are just waiting to hear them from you. When you pass along those terms during the phone interview, it confirms in their mind that you know what you're talking about, and possess the right knowledge base to be an effective expert on their case.

But, here's the thing: There are questions attorneys won't ask you outright. Instead, they will wait to hear you use certain words or phrases related to your industry. In my case, those terms include phrases like "best practices, industry standards, shoring certificates, and soil classes A, B, C, and D."

I was recently interviewed by a very pleasant attorney from Texas, on a trench-collapse case that resulted in a tragic death. As the attorney was giving me the nuts and bolts of the case, I was not just listening; I was also asking him questions—*loaded questions*—designed to convey my particular expertise or knowledge about my field.

Why not just offer him the information I knew he was seeking, but wouldn't ask me for directly?

There was a good reason for this: If I began spouting off a bunch of random knowledge, it would come across as bragging. By offering the information in the form of questions, I was able to give the attorney the buzzwords he was looking for without coming across as arrogant.

I learned the hard way just how important it was to convey my expertise to an attorney interviewing me—even if he didn't ask for it—*without giving away the store.*

It was my very first phone interview that taught me that lesson.

Here's what happened: As the attorney described the case, I listened intently, not saying very much. There were distinct pauses by the attorney, where it is clear to me now that he was waiting for a comment from me. I resisted commenting until I heard as much as the attorney was willing to divulge.

I then offered my initial opinions in great detail, being careful to say, "I would need to see all the evidence before I could form any final opinion or conclusion."

I remember that phone interview like it was yesterday. It did not result in me getting hired, and it left me thinking I might have offered too lengthy and detailed an initial opinion.

After all, the attorney picked my brain, and I provided him with a lot of initial observations and opinions. So, it stands to reason that he may very well have picked the brains of *several* expert witnesses, taking a little bit of information from each of them—without ever hiring any of them, or paying them for their expertise.

There is no way for me to be certain what happened during that initial phone call. What I do know is that an expert needs to be careful not to provide too detailed an initial opinion, or divulge too much information, during the attorney interview. You can give away free samples, so to speak, but that's where it ends. After all, you get paid for your knowledge and experience.

Here is the balance that needs to be struck: You should provide your initial observations and opinions, without going into great detail as to *why* you feel that way. That is what an attorney is going to pay for—the "why" behind your opinion.

As more attorney interviews followed, I found that the process was virtually the same each time. By now, I had learned when it was appropriate to reply, and how much to disclose.

One last note: *The demeanor you present in attorney interviews is as important as the information you provide.*

You want to be consistent—conveying knowledge in your field, as well as confidence and professionalism. Perhaps most importantly of all, you want to make sure to sound convincing. If you don't sound convincing during the initial attorney interview, the attorney will not believe you stand a chance of being convincing when it really counts—in your report and during deposition or trial testimony.

• **Anticipating Attorney's Interview Questions**

There will undoubtedly be questions in every initial attorney interview that you cannot anticipate in advance. There are certain common questions, however, that are likely to come up. Below, I provide some of those questions, along with possible responses geared towards your experience level.

Of course, as I said in the disclaimers at the beginning of this book, every situation is unique, and these responses should only be used as a guide; they should not necessarily be used, verbatim.

Question: How long have you been a practicing expert witness?

Response:

If you are a new expert, just starting your practice, simply state how long you've been practicing, and include the time it took to set up your practice. After all, you didn't just flip a switch one day, and say, "Voila! Now I'm an expert witness."

You did your research, set up a system, and read many books on the subject (including this one). The entire process likely took several months. So use that set-up time to your advantage, by including it in your statement about the length of time you've been practicing as an expert witness. This will instantly add experience and seasoning to your qualifications.

If you are an experienced expert witness, you might want to say, "Sir, I have been a practicing expert witness for X number of years now. I am very experienced and have had several cases. There are some case summaries and a list of attorney references on my website."

Then, ask the caller whether they have had the opportunity to visit your website. This is important. If the attorney has visited your website, they may not have taken the time to explore it. If they have not, you want them to visit it.

You will recall that in chapter three, we discussed the importance of a professionally designed website. It is something to take pride in! And, it will become one of your best marketing tools.

Question: Have you ever testified in court?
Response:

The attorney knows that everyone must start somewhere. He did! I'm sure he remembers his very first case, and how grateful he was to get it. So, just be candid.

If you are a brand new expert, and have just started your practice, keep your answer short and simple. Say, "Sir, I just started my expert witness practice X months ago, so I have not yet had the opportunity to testify in court." Don't elaborate. You don't want to highlight the point, and thereby give it additional importance or weight.

While the attorney may have called you looking for someone experienced, he may end up retaining you, based upon the knowledge and confidence you express during the interview.

If, on the other hand, you are a brand new, inexperienced expert, but you have testified in court as a *fact witness*—either for your own company, or for someone else—simply say, "Yes, Sir. I have testified in court." Don't elaborate. A simple yes will do.

If you are a relatively new, minimally experienced expert, but you have not yet had an opportunity to testify in court, because the cases you've worked on have all resulted in settlement, you could say, "I have had X number of cases, which have all settled out of court."

Question: How many times have you testified?
Response:

(For brand new experts, this has been covered in the above section.)

If you are an experienced expert, simply provide the number of times, if any, you have appeared in court: "Sir, I have had X number of cases, but have only had to go to trial one time. I like to think my expert reports had an impact on inducing settlement in the other cases I have had."

Attorneys know full well that between 94% and 97% percent of all cases settle, and never see the inside of a courtroom.

Question: What are your fees? Law 12/18
Response:

Many new experts get a bit nervous about this question, but there is no need. As discussed in the beginning of this book, it takes years to develop and hone your expertise. Your extensive experience—and your time—are valuable!

Once you have done your research, determined the range of fees your peers are commanding, and set an appropriate fee for your own services, you should state your fee with confidence.

When asked about your fees, simply say, "My fee is $$$.$$ per hour, and I also charge for other normal and customary expenses. And, I charge $$$.$$ for time spent by my research assistant(s)." (Most expert witnesses charge a lesser fee for time spent by assistants.)

Take this opportunity to tell the attorney that you will email them your retainer agreement, which details your fee structure. This accomplishes two major things: It provides the permission you need to email marketing materials to the attorney. And, more importantly, it provides the very document the attorney needs to retain your services.

Question: Do you have a staff?
Response:

As mentioned in Chapter Five, having a staff is not a requirement for an expert witness. However, having a staff *does* tend to create a positive impression.

Remember, expert witnesses who have research assistants on staff, for example, generally charge less than their expert hourly rate for time spent by their research assistant(s). This is good business practice, as well as a good selling point.

If you do not have a research assistant, you should simply say, "I do all the work myself. I do not have a staff. However, I would like to point out that I charge $$$.$$ less per hour when I am only doing research or clerical tasks."

This puts you on a par with experts who offer discounted fees for time spent by their staff.

This is good business practice, and it will help in your retention percentage (the number of times you are retained by the attorneys who call to consider your services).

Question: What percentage of the cases on which you've been retained have been on the side of the plaintiff, and what percentage on the side of the defendant? (For example, maybe 60% plaintiff/40% defendant, or the other way around.)

Response:

This question seems insignificant, but it is not. If your case history is very lopsided, and you opine more often on behalf of either the plaintiff or the defendant, you may be labeled as biased for one side or the other.

In my experience, you do not need to be overly concerned with this—nor will you be able to fully control which side retains you. But, to the extent you are able, try to keep the balance as even as possible.

I try to maintain no more than a 20% variance between plaintiff and defendant cases. 50%—50% is ideal, but 60%—40% is also fine. If you notice you are getting to a point where you're doing more like 70%—30% or 80%—20%, you will need to be prepared to be questioned about this imbalance.

Here is the type of question that can arise: "So, Mr. Expert, I see that you testify 80% of the time for the plaintiff. So it is fair to say that you are sympathetic to the plaintiff. Isn't that true?"

If you find yourself in that situation, you can say, "No, Counselor, I am called at random by attorneys representing both plaintiffs and defendants. I do not control who contacts me. I only accept cases where my specific field of expertise is required, and applicable to the case. I base my opinion on the evidence—not on whether or not I have been retained by counsel for the plaintiff or the defendant."

This answer defuses the implication that you show favoritism.

• Avoiding Premature Opinions and Conclusions

During these interviews, the attorney will spoon-feed you certain facts of the case. It is important to keep in mind that, generally speaking, these are the facts that tend to support the position of the attorney or their client. It is impossible—unethical, even—to form firm and final opinions or a conclusion at this stage.

Yet, the attorney will try to get a feel for the position you are likely to take—favorable or unfavorable to *their* position. After all, an attorney would not want to hire an expert whose opinion was likely to be dramatically opposed to theirs.

I always explain to the attorney that it is my job as an expert to evaluate the facts and evidence, and form my opinions and conclusion based on them. I use the following qualifying statement: "Based on the facts you have given me, it is likely, or unlikely, that…"

Two things can't be said enough. One—under no circumstances can you, or should you, ever form a firm conclusion before you have seen the actual evidence. Two—you should always alert the retaining counsel to all the evidence you uncover, both that which is likely, *and that which is unlikely*, to support his position.

If you discover unfavorable evidence, call the attorney directly, and explain the circumstances thoroughly, and in detail. That way, the attorney has full knowledge of anything that might be unfavorable to his case, and he can prepare accordingly.

It is far worse to try to hide anything negative you might find. It is bound to come out in the end, and when it does, the case—and your credibility—will suffer.

Remember, your job is not to support your client's position, with disregard to the truth and the facts. Your job is to support the client's position *if, and only if,* the facts support doing so. And if they don't, they don't.

You should never go into a courtroom or deposition and state a certain opinion, (or state one in your report) unless it can be supported.

• **Fixing a Deadline for Open Files**

After the initial attorney interview, I do not wait indefinitely for the attorney to decide whether or not to retain me. It is my personal policy to inform the attorney—over the phone, and then in a follow-up email—that I only keep a file open for fifteen calendar days.

The reason I do this is twofold. First, it puts the attorney in a position where they need to make a decision, one way or another, about retaining me. Secondly, as long as I maintain an open file on a case, I am technically prohibited from speaking to opposing counsel on the same case.

It is important to note that, just as you will be spoon-fed favorable evidence about the case by the attorney interviewing you, his opposing counsel might be in possession of evidence that would support the exact opposite position. You don't want to put yourself in a position where you have to turn down a case from opposing counsel, simply because you already have an open file on the case.

You should be aware of a tactic used by some attorneys that is unofficially known by expert witnesses as "blocking out." It involves the hiring of experts for the sole purpose of preventing the opposition from retaining them. An expert cannot serve both sides in a case—and that, in itself, gives rise to the practice.

For example, there was a recent catastrophic oil rig explosion that resulted in thousands of gallons of crude oil spewing into the Gulf of Mexico, from an oil rig owned by a major oil company. The oil company responsible for the disaster attempted to hire hundreds, if not thousands, of marine biologists and scientists.

A Huffington Post article written on the subject discussed how the oil company attempted to hire the entire marine biology department of a major southern university!

Why would they do such a thing? The answer is found in the retainer agreements the oil company was attempting to get the research scientists to sign— agreements which placed substantial restrictions on what the scientists could publish, share, *or even discuss*. The oil company claimed that they had the following reasons for placing such restrictions on the scientists:

It was in the best interests of scientific study;

It was for the purpose of determining what went wrong; and

It was necessary in order to determine how to repair the problem and prevent it in the future.

Here is the reality: The experts who agreed to sign the contract limiting their ability to discuss the disaster *would be unavailable to thousands and thousands of litigants and their legal counsel.*

That is a large-scale example of blocking out. Obviously, the practice also occurs on a much smaller scale. Let's say an attorney has interviewed you, and you've opened a file on the case, containing the names of the players and circumstances. Several months go by, and the attorney does not get back to you.

Isn't he preventing you from being available to the opposing counsel, and effectively blocking you out, at no cost to him? Yes he is.

Of course, if you confronted such an attorney, and asked him if he was engaging in the practice of "blocking out," he would likely deny it, claiming, "Not at all—we are still looking around, and interviewing various experts."

There may be many perfectly ethical reasons why an attorney who interviews you fails to make a decision, or get back in touch with you. Whatever the reason, however, he has effectively accomplished the same thing that the oil company accomplished— blocking out a witness—without having to pay a penny.

48 Laws
Law 8: pg 62

By limiting the time you keep a file open, you will force an attorney into making a decision. Should they opt not to retain you, you would then be available to the opposing counsel, if they happened to call. You may, or may not, want to enter into an agreement with opposing counsel, but by advising the initial attorney who contacted you of your intention to close the file within a set period of time, you are leaving your options open.

In the email I send to attorneys, advising them that I only keep a file open for fifteen calendar days, I also state in clear language that I have not yet reviewed any hard evidence. This is a protection for me, in the event the attorney tries to claim that I am privy to confidential information, and thereby prevented from working for opposing counsel.

If opposing counsel happens to call—either before or after I've closed my file on the initial attorney interview—I advise him that I have been contacted by his opposition, but I have not been retained. I explain that the first attorney has told me some of the circumstances and facts of the case, but I have not received any evidence to support the information divulged to me during that conversation. Lastly, I tell him whether the file is open or closed, and if it is still open, how long it will remain open.

To be clear, there is no way I would allow, or participate in, a discussion with opposing counsel in which I divulged the confidential conversation I had with the first attorney. Any discussion must be confined to the facts and circumstances the new attorney is revealing to me.

• Accepting Your First Case

My first case was referred to me by a referral agency. They found me through a search of their database. Provided I was hired by their client (the attorney), I would be billing the agency, and they would be sending an invoice to the attorney.

The agency sent me an email, advising me that I might be receiving a phone call from an attorney who wanted to interview me for a case. In the email, I was instructed to avoid discussing fees, because the agency's fee is added to my fee when they bill the client.

The next thing I knew, I got a call from the plaintiff's attorney.

The case was a David-versus-Goliath situation. The dispute involved a relatively small rental company (the plaintiff in the case), which rented heavy equipment to a general contractor performing border wall construction in New Mexico. The rental company was owed in excess of $1.2 million by the general contractor—a large international firm, whose subcontractor had gone out of business.

The attorney provided me with enough factual information for me to get a sense of whether or not I was qualified to opine on the case. On his end, he was listening for several key things in my reply. First, he was trying to get a sense of my knowledge, experience, and expertise. He was also trying to get a read on whether or not I was likely to generally agree with his position, given the facts he presented to me. Of course, he was also listening for intangibles, such as professionalism and demeanor.

We talked briefly about some of the facts of the case, and my thoughts and feelings about those facts. During that initial phone interview, I only evaluated the general circumstances, and determined whether I was qualified to opine on them, based upon my experience and qualifications. At that level, I had not yet formed opinions or a conclusion.

The next phone call I received was from the actual client of the attorney, who wanted to interview me personally. I would later discover that such an occurrence was somewhat unusual. The next thing I knew, I was hired.

I had only been given a brief synopsis of the case, a thumbnail sketch of the parties to the lawsuit, and the nature of the dispute. I had not yet seen a single piece of evidence. I had no way of knowing that there would be hundreds of thousands of pages to review!

Once I was hired, I told him, "Be sure to send me all the evidence, not just what you think I need, or what you believe may apply to my expertise."

Here are the two reasons why I said that:

First of all, I needed to catalog every piece of evidence received, and include it as part of my report. If there were, for example, twenty depositions in the case, but the attorney only sent me ten, I could only catalog ten, review ten, and form my opinions based upon those ten.

When I got to deposition or trial, the very first thing the opposing counsel would say to me was, "You have catalogued ten depositions here, but there are actually twenty. That means you have not reviewed the other ten, right?"

I would have to reply, "That is correct, sir. I did not review the other ten."

"So, Mr. Gulya," the attorney would continue, "there may be evidence in those ten depositions that could change your opinion, right?"

I would have no choice but to say, "It's possible. I would have to read them before I could say for certain."

Of course, such things can always be addressed during re-direct examination. But, my initial statement that I might have changed my opinion if I'd seen all the documents leaves a bad impression with the jury. It also places doubt in their eyes as to the accuracy or reliability of my report.

Secondly, no attorney is going to be familiar with my particular field of expertise. So, they may not know what I would consider relevant, and might inadvertently decide to exclude some critical piece of evidence.

- **Understanding How Attorney/Client Privilege Pertains to You**

There is another reason why an attorney might withhold evidence from an expert: In most cases, all confidential attorney/client communications become discoverable *the minute they are handed over to an expert.*

Let's say a party to a lawsuit sent an email to his attorney (who then retained you as an expert on the case), and the email said, "Listen, just between you and me, I think you should know, I was not really wearing my seatbelt!"

Such an email is not necessarily discoverable, because it is protected under attorney/client privilege. However, it *could* be used as evidence if it were to be made public. So, if the attorney sends it to you, the same email that should have fallen under attorney/client privilege protection may be now discoverable.

The reality is, you can only base your opinions and conclusion on the discovery evidence you have been given. If an attorney chooses not to send you a protected piece of evidence, opposing counsel is not going to have seen it either, because it was not discoverable.

You won't even know that piece of evidence exists—and neither will opposing counsel—so it becomes a moot point.

• **Handling Large Quantities of Evidence**

Some cases have as little as fifty to one hundred pages of documents for an expert to review, while other have thousands. When you have thousands of pages to review, they all need to be properly and efficiently documented, cataloged, and evaluated. With voluminous cases, there are thousands of details, all potentially significant—and, as the saying goes, "The devil is in the details."

As mentioned above, I was sent in excess of a hundred thousand pages of evidence on my very first case.

My report ended up being fifty-six pages in length. (Most of my reports to follow would turn out to be around twenty-five to thirty pages.)

Dealing with all those documents requires a qualified and trained assistant. My assistant had to carefully catalog each page. We started by scanning each page into a database, using a high volume scanner, whereby we then added tags, keywords, Bates numbers, and other identifiers. While this was time consuming work up front, it saved countless hours of my expert, billable labor later in the process.

A detailed catalog was instantly generated and updated, including a compact disc (CD), which linked to the actual PDF-scanned documents.

Upon completion of this process, I was able to pull up any document, and see links to related documents and exhibits instantly. One click, and any document I wanted to see was instantly before my eyes, without hunting or searching through file after file of hard copies.

Handling voluminous evidence in this way assures accurate, detailed analysis and review of the documents—and does so in an efficient manner. It also allows for fast and accurate citing of evidence during the expert report writing process.

If you find yourself with thousands of documents, I highly recommend that you implement this method.

• **Establishing Your Own Work System**

It didn't take long to realize that my first case was going to be rather complex. I had written many things over the course of my lifetime—letters, proposals, and correspondence to attorneys related to legal matters. Writing an expert report was going to be a brand new experience. I was both nervous and excited to get started.

By this point, I had read instructive books about becoming an expert, and I had a basic understanding of how to prepare the report, and what I needed to include in it. However, every expert report is different and unique, and, when it comes to formats, there are as many variations as there are experts. I would need to develop my own style, while making sure I included all the components necessary and required by the court.

I began receiving voluminous amounts of evidence—eighty cartons in total, sent to me little by little. Included were eight-hundred-page depositions, hundreds of letters between the parties, rental receipts and invoices, and an email stream containing thousands of emails. It was critical that I had an accurate way to track all the time that was going to be required to pore over the evidence.

I quickly realized I needed to establish a working system for myself. Step one—finding software that would help me properly track, document, and bill my time. I was being paid by the hour, and the sheer volume of the material told me that this was going to be a time-consuming job.

So, I went out and purchased the appropriate software. The time-tracking/record-keeping software I bought has a timer and billing capabilities.

This type of software ranges in price from modest to very, very expensive. I decided upon—and recommend—the lower-priced software. It performs all the necessary functions, has a timer, and calculates your billable rates for multiple users, such as research assistants and clerical personnel. It factors in all of those things, and then generates an invoice you can send to your clients.

More importantly, this type of software—both the low-end and high-end versions—is widely utilized by the legal community. This could become important if you were ever challenged about the amount of billable time you have invoiced. It makes a far better impression if you are able to tell them you are using a recognized version of legal software, as opposed to, let's say, a wristwatch.

It is important to note that I would *never* accept a case on a fixed-fee basis, and, in fact, I have turned down cases where the attorney said to me in the initial interview, "Listen, we are willing to pay you X amount of money, regardless of whether it takes you two hours or two hundred."

I will always reject a case offered to me on that basis—not due to greed, but due to the fact that I cannot possibly provide the best service to a client when a restriction is placed on how many hours I am allowed to spend on the case.

I bill in the neighborhood of $285.00—385.00/hour and I charge for every notebook and paper I print. I also charge for time spent by research assistants (at the rate of $120.00/hour), and for all other expenses. My approach to billing is very similar to the way attorneys bill their clients.

• Making an Impact

My first case demonstrated to me the impact my opinion could have on the outcome. As you will recall, the dispute involved a rental company, which rented heavy equipment to a contractor performing border wall construction in New Mexico.

Here's what happened: By virtue of the Miller Act, as well as their payment-and-performance bond, the general contractor was liable for the debt of the subcontractor they hired. When they received the rental company's demand for payment, the general contractor alleged that the company had charged in excess of fair value for the rentals.

After extensive research and analysis, I was of the opinion that the rental company had not overcharged, as alleged by the general contractor.

My report was instrumental in the case settling out of court.

• Dealing with Emotional Content

While my first case gave me experience dealing with a tremendous volume of evidence, a subsequent case was a lesson in highly emotional and intense content. It involved the tragic death of a construction worker, who was horrifically buried alive by a trench collapse. The accident was covered on TV by the local news.

I was retained by the attorney for the defendant— the company for which the decedent worked.

I was sent a CD with photos from the accident scene. Those were bad enough; the graphic autopsy photos I was sent were even worse. I wasn't expecting to receive them, and found them very disturbing. The evidence also included hundreds of other photos, a description of the type of shoring used, fifteen lengthy depositions, CAL-OSHA investigative reports, fire, police, and rescue reports, citations, and thirty-thousand pages of other documents and evidence.

This case would test my ability to remain analytical in the face of moving emotional content.

The depositions from the decedent/plaintiff's side of the case were highly emotional. Reading the description of the disaster that caused the decedent's death, my heart went out to the wife who had lost her husband, and the kids who had lost their father, while he was still so young and in the prime of his life.

All of those aspects of the case were heartbreaking. But they did not change the *facts* of the case, and they did not change the fact that my opinions and conclusion needed to be responsive to this question: Was something done improperly or incorrectly by the company or other workers that caused this disaster to happen?

I could—and did—feel deeply sorry for the family's loss, but my emotional response did not mean that the company or the workers had acted improperly. Until I finished reviewing all the evidence, I had no idea what my opinions and conclusion would be.

After a thorough review of all the documentation, depositions, and other evidence, I provided an initial sixty-page expert report, as well as a twenty-five-page supplemental report, including test results, graphs, charts, and a detailed analysis.

My opinion was as follows:

It appeared that the company did, in fact, train the workers, and provide them with the necessary tools and equipment to do their job correctly, according to best practices and industry standards.

It was also my opinion that, although the workers did not perform their job one-hundred-percent by the book, the amount of inconsistency was so miniscule, it would not have caused the outcome—the trench collapse that caused this man's death.

My conclusion: Despite its tragic nature, the worker's death was caused by other factors.

The case settled, and the client stated, "Mr. Gulya, your reports were excellent! They were detailed, accurate, and professional, and proved to be instrumental and central in settling this case. Thank you!"

I was on my way to becoming a renowned site-work construction expert.

~ 6 ~

COMMUNICATION
Your Report

*"An expert is someone who has succeeded in making
decisions and judgments simpler
through knowing what to pay attention to
and what to ignore."*
~ Edward de Bono

• **Developing Your Own Style**

An expert witness is responsible for both written
and verbal communication. Long before you are ever
deposed, or required to give your oral testimony in a
courtroom setting, you will be preparing your written
report. As I said, there are as many different ways to
prepare your report as there are expert witnesses.

I have never read a book that specifies one particular way an expert report should be organized and
formatted. "Writing and Defending Your Report" is
one of the best, most well-known books on the subject, yet even it does not spell out the precise way
that an expert must write their report. It suggests

certain language, and instructs the reader to make their report neat, professional, grammatically correct, and so on.

I am also unaware of any federal, state, or civil requirements or regulations governing the *formatting or organizing* of an expert witness report.

Of course, the (state or) Federal Rules of Civil Procedure state that certain *content* must be included in an expert witness report, but they do not dictate the way in which that content must be presented.

When it comes to your report, I believe that most things are a matter of preference. There may be more than one way to do something properly, and it is simply a matter of trial and error, until you learn which method works best for you.

- **Preliminary Opinion versus Final Opinions and Conclusion**

The minute I start reading through the evidence (which may come to me out of chronological order), I begin forming the rough draft of an outline.

I make personal notes to jog my memory later on. A note to myself might be along the lines of, *Okay, I don't yet know all the circumstances and evidence, but page thirty-two of Mr. X's deposition looks important, and you're going to want to refer back to it later.*

Using that trench collapse case as an example, my first thought was, *This poor guy. What a tragedy!*

It bears repeating—I was not retained to evaluate the level of tragedy related to the accident that took the decedent's life. I was hired to evaluate whether or not the trench shoring was installed correctly or incorrectly, and what responsibility, if any, the company may have had in the accident.

I couldn't deny or eliminate the tragic nature of the circumstances. Any human being with a heart would have had sympathy for the decedent, and his bereaved wife and family. That did not mean that those initial feelings and thoughts belonged in my report. It was possible that they would eventually show up in my report similarly worded, but only once I had reviewed and digested all the factual evidence.

At first, I reasoned, *Well, the evidence shows that OSHA cited the company. Taking into consideration all the details surrounding this case, the company may have problems here. After all, this poor guy was buried alive, and died!*

But, such thoughts were too preliminary to comprise my formal opinions or conclusion. Personal beliefs do not become factual opinions until I know all the facts of the case.

• Organizing Your Report

As I have already stated, there is no hard and fast rule in terms of the format for your report. But, regardless of the facts of any particular case, or the conclusion one might draw from them, the *organization* of those facts is important. You wouldn't want to scatter a bunch of facts in no particular order.

To some degree, it is important to keep the facts in chronological order. More importantly, you want to keep the facts grouped according to theme, and try to remain somewhat consistent.

Overall, I think a report is best constructed through an organization of facts that lead up to the important opinions and conclusion.

Here is what I do: First, I read all the evidence and take copious notes. Just as with a story or novel, the plot builds. The more I read, the more I am able to understand the characters, and the more I gather from the circumstances and environment.

By the time I have gone through all the evidence, I have read the book, so to speak, and begun to form in my mind a synopsis of what happened, why it happened, and whether the players did—or did not do— what they should have done, given the particular set of circumstances.

By this point, I have drawn a preliminary opinion and conclusion that either does, or does not, support the position of the client on whose behalf I was retained. Now, I am ready to prepare my report.

I read or heard somewhere that people tend to remember the very first thing, and the very last thing, they read. So, I arrange my reports in such a way that the first thing a jury encounters in my report is the background—a synopsis of the case. In the middle, I place all the facts, figures, charts, and graphs. While the jury may read the information in the middle, they may not necessarily pay a great deal of attention to it.

I build my report with facts, and then my opinions, and then, ultimately, my final conclusion. As my facts build, I keep more toward the end of the report whatever I consider the strongest, most convincing facts, as they relate to my ultimate opinions and conclusion. In this way, I am supporting my position as I build.

That way, when the jury gets to the last two pages, all of the background they remember from the beginning of the report starts to make sense, because I've saved the strongest part of my report for last.

- **Familiarizing Yourself with The Federal Rules of Civil Procedure**

The Federal Rules of Civil Procedure (hereafter, I will be calling them The Rules) govern what is, and is not, discoverable in a legal proceeding.

The Rules underwent important reform in December of 2010. The new Rules have placed new limitations on what an opposing counsel can obtain from expert witness files. It is essential that experts familiarize themselves with these changes, so they will have a clear understanding of how The Rules affect their practice.

Let me explain why it is imperative that you have a full understanding of these changes. First, a little history lesson.

Prior to 1993, parties were generally limited to traditional discovery methods (such as interrogatories) in obtaining information from opposing parties, including information regarding testifying experts.

Then, in 1993, Rule 26 of The Rules was amended. The amendment stated, in part, that an expert's report must disclose all data and other information *"considered"* by the witness in forming his or her opinions. By definition, the term *"considered"* is all-inclusive, as opposed to the term *"relied upon,"* which was previously used. This one-word change was very significant.

The 1993-amended Rule 26 was interpreted by courts to require experts to disclose *all* documents the expert generated, or examined, in the process of forming their opinions. This included all draft reports and notes, as well as any evidence where the expert may have jotted a note in a margin or highlighted a sentence.

In December of 2010, The Rules once again underwent sweeping reform. Of particular importance: Expert's draft reports are no longer discoverable.

During the period of time in which an expert's draft reports *were* still considered discoverable (before the December 2010 changes to The Rules), experts were put in a position where they had to avoid draft reports at all costs. Otherwise, they were subject to unfair scrutiny by attorneys, who would take an expert's draft report, extract a sentence or paragraph, and say, "But in this draft, you said X, and now you're saying Y!"

Attorneys did this, knowing full well that a draft is meant to be an outline only, not a final version of an expert's opinion or conclusion.

Then you'd have to explain that it was a draft—raw, unpolished, and incomplete in terms of what you ultimately wanted to say. Having to go through such arduous explanations wasted time for everyone—the court, the jurors, the attorneys, and the expert.

Experts are now free to create drafts, knowing that there is protection for drafts of any report, regardless of the form in which the draft is recorded. Communications between experts and attorneys are also protected now, regardless of the form of the communication.

Of course, you should consult with the retaining attorney concerning any expert witness/attorney communication requested during discovery by the opposing counsel. That gives the retaining attorney the opportunity to object to requests made by the opposing counsel for files or documents. The court will then decide what the opposition is, or is not, entitled to receive from the expert, based on The Rules.

To summarize:

Prior to 1993, The Rules had provided work product protection to testifying experts;

The 1993 amendments allowed for almost total discoverability of every document, communication, and draft the expert had in their file;

The 2010 change to Rule 26 is an attempt to strike a balance between the 1993 "all things are discoverable" mentality, and the pre-1993 rules, which limited production of expert's files to traditional discovery methods such as interrogatories; and

The 2010 amended Rules clarify the protection of certain types of communications between experts and retaining counsel. This is vitally important to experts.

Experts will continue to be subject to all Rule 26 requirements. Because some states have variations of The Rules, the expert should consult The Rules for the state in which the case is being tried, for any deviation between the state's rules and the federal rules.

Assuming no state variations in the federal rules, however, one of the requirements of an expert is that they disclose their fee schedule in their report. In certain states, it is not a requirement.

If I am going to err, I prefer to err on the side of safety, so I do it as a matter of course. Every single report I produce contains my fee or retainer agreement schedule. I don't want to have someone come to me and say, "You didn't put your fee schedule in your report!"

There are circumstances in which I believe less is more—but this isn't one of them. I believe it is best to develop the habit of including your fee schedule in your report.

I also believe in including standardized elements in all of your reports. That way, you can always say, "My reports contain X, Y, and Z elements, regardless of whether or not they are required by state civil procedure." Those might include a catalog of evidence, your fee schedule, and the abbreviated version of your CV.

Attorneys are then aware that it's your policy that every report you write will contain those items—regardless of the state in which the case is being tried.

The retaining attorney can always come to you and specifically ask you to remove one of your standard items from your report, if he cares to do so. At that point, you can take it out. But, choosing to leave things out can give the appearance that you are either hiding things, or you're inconsistent.

- **Supporting Your Content with Demonstrative Evidence** *Law 9, Pg. 69*

What is demonstrative evidence? It is evidence outside of normal discovery—documentation the expert produces to prove and support their opinions and conclusion. Examples: Graphs, charts, exhibits, x-rays, diagrams, DVD's, CD's, and detailed copies of rules or regulations.

If you are going to use it (and you should, where applicable), it needs to support your opinions and conclusion, and demonstrate how you arrived at them. You don't want to include a graph or pie chart simply because it looks official. It needs to support something you've opined on, and drawn a conclusion about.

For example, if there is an OSHA regulation that pertains to the case I'm working on, I need to take that data directly out of OSHA, word for word, print it out, and make it an exhibit in my report.

Demonstrative evidence is a critical part of your report. Every opinion and conclusion you form must be based on supporting documentation, and that documentation needs to be part and parcel of your report.

Your demonstrative evidence, and discovery evidence, forms the foundation for your report. Without it, you have a house of cards.

Here's an example. Let's say, I state, "John Smith said, 'At no time did I ever install the shoring incorrectly.'" The fact that John Smith said something under oath, and under penalty of perjury, does not preclude his statement from being false or misleading.

I cannot simply base my opinions on something Mr. Smith said. I must support my use of Mr. Smith's statement with demonstrative evidence, and other supporting evidence.

• Understanding Rebuttal Reports

A rebuttal report varies in format from an original report, in that it specifically addresses what the opposing counsel's expert has opined on. This kind of report comes into play after you have already reviewed the evidence, rendered your opinions and conclusion, and submitted your report. The objective of a rebuttal report is to rebut—or show why—the other expert's opinions and conclusion are misleading, erroneous, or without factual support.

Perhaps the opposition's expert did not utilize demonstrative evidence—or cite his source (such as deposition testimony). That should be pointed out in a rebuttal report. An expert's opinion, without supporting evidence, is not worth the paper it's printed on. You should seize the opportunity to diminish the opposing expert's credibility when appropriate.

Or, let's say the opposition's expert utilized *your* demonstrative evidence, and cherry-picked the parts of it that suited his time frame, date ranges, opinions, and conclusion. He might then claim to be using the data *you've supplied* as the supporting documentation for his conclusion that you are wrong—even though he is taking your demonstrative evidence out of context!

Or, perhaps he utilized his own demonstrative evidence, and came to a different conclusion than you did. What supporting documentation was used? Was it factual, based on truth, and not arrived at by taking your data, comments, or demonstrative evidence out of context? Those are the kinds of things to look for, and address, in a rebuttal report.

It is important that you discuss with retaining counsel your findings, observations, and conclusions regarding the opposing expert's report.

The retaining attorney may tell you, "I don't want to refute it at this time. Save that for deposition or trial." It is the attorney's call to make.

• Paying Attention to the Appearance of Your Report

I often receive from opposing counsel the reports of experts they have retained. As discussed above, I am sent these reports because there are times when opposing experts will mention my name in the context of, "Mr. Gulya stated that Mr. Smith did not do X, Y, or Z." I must always disclose any such reports received by me.

Whenever I read an expert's report that is disorganized, has a host of footnotes at the bottom, looks cluttered, or doesn't read well, I am reminded of the importance of appearance.

The use of footnotes, for example, is technically acceptable. But, often a jury is deciding the case, and ultimately, they are the ones who are going to read your report. You don't want a jury member to have to go on a hunting expedition to find what they are looking for in your report, because you've decided to include fifty footnotes.

In my estimation, it is better to include the support for what you are saying right in the text of the report. As for me, I cite evidence either using a Bates number, if that's how the document has been identified, or using page and line numbers, as well as the name of the discovery document to which it refers—e.g., page 13, line 6 of the deposition of Bob Miller.

I discuss citations in depth in the section below.

• Citations and Your Credibility

A citation is commonly defined as a reference to a published or unpublished source (not necessarily the original source).

More precisely, "a citation is an abbreviated alphanumeric expression …embedded in the body of an intellectual work that denotes an entry in the bibliographic references section of the work for the purpose of acknowledging the relevance of the works of others to the topic of discussion at the spot where the citation appears." (Author unknown, **http://en. wikipedia.org/wiki/Citation**).

Generally, the combination of both the in-body citation, and the bibliographic entry, constitute what is universally considered a citation.

The primary purpose of a citation is intellectual honesty—to attribute to other authors the ideas they have previously expressed, rather than give the appearance to the reader that something is the author's original idea.

Whether you have been an expert witness for years, or are just starting out, accurate research, proper formatting of citations, and clarity will make your written report accurate, impressive and, most of all, credible. As you gain experience in proper techniques, you will become more confident and comfortable using citations.

The form of citations generally conforms to one of the generally accepted citations systems, such as the Harvard, MLA, or APA (American Psychological Association). These citation systems have their respective advantages and disadvantages relative to the tradeoffs of being informative, but not too disruptive.

It is essential to recognize that each of the various types of citations, and reference listing styles, has a specific format that must be followed. Be sure to cite your resources and references in the proper format, e.g., Harvard, MLA, or APA. This will ensure that your report is clear, concise and credible. In my opinion, the APA is generally acceptable for expert reports, but any of the three mentioned above would be completely acceptable.

Perhaps the most efficient format of all, however, is the Bates Stamp. Bates numbering is commonly used as an organizational method of labeling and identifying legal documents. During the discovery phase of litigation, a large number of documents might necessitate the use of unique identifiers for each page of each document, for reference and retrieval purposes. Bates numbering (named for the Bates automatic numbering machine) assigns an arbitrary, unique identifier to each page. The "numbering" may be solely numeric, or may contain a combination of letters and numbers (alphanumeric), for example, Bates #XYZ000123.

There are many free citation builders available online—but the free versions do have limitations. There will, however, often be upgrades available that you can pay to obtain. Citation builders assure correct formatting of Harvard, APA, and other citation formats.

One such citation builder is SourceAid.com, which has a free version, and upgrades at an additional cost. Sourceaid.com is available on a term basis of two weeks, three months, or one year.

• Avoiding Common Citation Mistakes

One of the most common mistakes I see when analyzing my counterparts' expert reports has to do with the improper formatting of references and citations. This frequently results in unsubstantiated or misleading conclusions, and will assuredly be red-flagged by opposing counsel—who will rigorously question you about it during cross-examination.

The questioning will be harsh, and deliberately targeted to reduce your credibility, and bring it into doubt in the eyes of the judge and/or jury. Once doubt is injected into the jury's mind, your report, testimony, opinions, and conclusion become questionable, at best, and at worst, unreliable and unbelievable.

I have also seen opposition expert's reports that are entirely devoid of any citations or references. This is a critical error, and can result in cross-examination Armageddon for the expert witness.

So, if you are stating a fact or opinion, always check and cite your reference and source correctly. You want to leave no question about what is provable fact, your opinion, or supporting opinions of others.

The common definition of fact vs. opinion is this: Facts are *objective*. A fact can be proven, verified, and backed up with evidence. Opinions are *subjective*. An opinion is based on a belief or view, and expresses a preference or bias. It is not based on evidence that can be verified.

To check whether or not something is a fact, ask yourself, *Can this statement be proven, and would it be true all of the time?* To check whether or not something is an opinion, ask yourself, *Does this statement relate to a thought or feeling?*

There are key words you can look for which will give you a clue as to whether something is a fact or opinion—words like feel, believe, always, never, none, most, least, best, and worst.

Citing your sources correctly and professionally will eliminate any doubt as to your credibility, your integrity, and the accuracy of your expert report.

• **Making it Professional**

It is important to do your best to make your reports as polished, professional, and grammatically correct as possible.

Most people are not going to notice, or care about, small errors related to punctuation or grammar, and they are not going to expect you to be an English professor. On the other hand, if your reports are well-organized, but contain a bunch of improperly formatted, run-on, or fragmented sentences—or numerous misspelled words—it is going to reflect poorly on you. The reader is going to get the impression that either you are not on the ball, or you produce sloppy work.

Does that mean your reports need to be perfect? No. I'm not sure any expert writes perfect reports. As for me, I triple-proofread all my reports, catch as many mistakes as I can, and correct them. I aim for 100% perfection, but likely achieve 99% perfection.

• Making it Believable

My goal is to make my reports professional, truthful, convincing—*and believable to the average citizen who may be sitting on a jury*. So, I need to be truthful, and state the facts, as well as my opinions and conclusion, in a way that is convincing, and more importantly, believable.

When it comes to believability, length is key. Something has to be long enough to be believable—but if it is too long, it can seem like I am overselling the point. That can undermine the believability of the point I am trying to make.

If I can explain something in one paragraph, and make it clear, convincing, and believable, I don't need to take five paragraphs to do it. If it really does take five paragraphs, I need to take a closer look at how I'm phrasing my sentences.

Even though you want your report to be convincing and believable, you never want to sacrifice professionalism in the process. The minute you start meandering into emotionalism, you are in trouble.

My reports are always analytical. Even though I may have strong personal feelings that a certain regulation, for example, is right or wrong, it is what it is; it states what it states. I did not design it or write it; I just know what needs to be adhered to, and if it is not adhered to, what the results can be.

My expert witness report is not the proper arena for me to go on a rant, or expound upon my personal beliefs. I have been retained for one reason, and one reason only—to evaluate the evidence, and render my opinions and conclusion related thereto.

• Avoiding Absolutes

Here is a perfect example of an absolute statement: Never, ever use absolutes! In all seriousness, the use of absolute statements is one crucial pitfall you want to avoid in your reports.

As a rule, I don't state things in absolute terms, unless I am one-hundred-percent confident that it is indisputable—like my date of birth, for example. To avoid using absolutes, I use terms like, "To a reasonable degree of certainty or probability."

I have developed a personal scale that entails three forms of opinion:

One—absolute. This means that I am one-hundred-percent confident that it is indisputable. I rarely if ever use this form of opinion.

Two—reasonable certainty. This is something less than absolute but greater than merely probable.

Three—reasonable probability. This is less than reasonable certainty but still conceivable.

✗A newer expert may feel that they need to state their opinions or conclusion in absolute terms, but it is rare that anything is so absolute that there is not some set of circumstances that would change your opinion of that absolute.

I learned this through experience.

Here's what happened: When I was first starting my expert practice, I took a set of facts from a previous lawsuit in which my construction company had been involved. I reviewed depositions and other evidence of that nature. Then, I did a mock report, as if I were an expert witness retained on behalf of the construction company in that case.

For the writing of my expert report, I drew on all my reading and research, but it still came down to developing my own personal, individualized style.

I sent the mock report to Rosalie Hamilton, explaining that I had used actual facts from a case, in order to find my own system for organizing, formatting, and presenting reports. Rosalie forwarded it to an attorney friend of hers. He was more than happy to read it, vet it, and provide honest criticism.

He came back with what he did and did not like. Among the things he did not like was the fact that I drew absolute opinions and a conclusion, rather than using phrases like "reasonable certainty" or "reasonable probability." Everything was absolute—"the contractor did X, Y, and Z, and therefore I have reached this absolute conclusion."

I'm sure I could have found similar advice in the many how-to books written on the expert witness life, even if I had to search for it between the lines. But, it was so helpful to have the attorney review my mock report, and give me *personalized* advice.

He also engaged me in a mock question-and-answer session. Choosing a particular circumstance, and a particular opinion and conclusion I had stated related thereto, he led me through the kinds of questions an attorney was likely to ask me in deposition or trial.

In so doing, he showed me how my opinion could change as the circumstances changed. In this way, he was able to demonstrate to me the downfalls of using absolute statements. His input was invaluable to me.

- **Avoiding Use of Overstatements and Understatements**

Just as you want to avoid using absolutes, it is important to eliminate overstatements and understatements from your report. Overstatement words—very, certainly, and definitely, for example—tend to weaken the message and credibility of the expert.

It seems counterintuitive. One would think those types of words would enhance the forcefulness of the message, whether written or verbal. But, research shows that the opposite is actually true. These types of words are generally perceived by the listener as indicators of a lack of confidence and accuracy.

Whisper—don't shout.

Just as overstatement words undermine your credibility, so do understatement or "hedge" words and phrases. Here are some examples: sort of, kind of, maybe, probably, and likely.

Such words also indicate a lack of confidence, and give the reader or listener the impression that the writer, or speaker, is unsure of what they are saying.

Avoiding absolutes, overstatements, and understatements is as important in your oral testimony (see Testimony chapters below) as it is in your reports.

- **Having Your Report Reviewed Before Submitting it to Attorneys**

As you know by now, there are Rules of Civil Procedure governing your report, and you will need to review them as they pertain to this subject. But, generally speaking, if you are inclined to have someone review, edit, or proofread your report before submitting it to the retaining attorney, it is best to show it to someone on your own staff.

Having such things done in-house allows you to avoid the appearance of impropriety. You don't want an attorney saying to a jury, "You think this guy is so smart? Well, he had to send his report out to be edited by someone else. For that matter, how can we be sure all opinions and conclusions in the report are this expert's, and not that of the editor?"

Personally, I would rather have a misplaced comma or improper verb usage than have an attorney go down that road with me.

However, if you *must* have your report looked at by someone outside your own staff, be sure to redact the report—blacking out the names, parties to the suit, etc. And, make sure you reveal that fact to the retaining attorney.

No attorney wants to be caught by surprise by an expert who has engaged in behavior with even the *appearance* of impropriety.

~ 7 ~
TESTIMONY—PART ONE
Deposition

"A wise man is superior to any insults
which can be put upon him,
and the best reply to unseemly behavior
is patience and moderation."
~ Moliere

• Understanding Deposition Proceedings

Depositions are part of the fact-finding, discovery process, whereby plaintiffs and defendants gather information in preparation for trial. (In the United States, depositions are nearly always held outside of a courtroom setting.)

Generally speaking, they are conducted by attorneys. The opposing counsel will always be the one deposing you ("deposing counsel"). There may be several parties to the lawsuit, so there may be several attorneys present, but, regardless of how many attorneys are present, each one will have an opportunity to ask you questions.

During a deposition, a witness is questioned in order to produce oral testimony that will be reduced or converted to written form, for later use in court. Deposition participants generally include plaintiffs and defendants directly involved with the case, as well as witnesses, coworkers, and experts. As the deposition process evolves, the list of deponents can grow—and often does.

For example, if the plaintiff in a deposition mentions a name the attorneys have not heard before, they will make a note of the name, and later decide whether or not to depose that person.

It is important for an expert to recognize and understand that, although a deposition is not held in a court of law, it is conducted like a court proceeding. The expert is sworn in, and promises to tell the truth, the whole truth, and nothing but the truth. Your answers are admissible in a court of law.

The deposition process can be a very lengthy, grueling, and trying process for the expert. Knowing what to expect, and being fully prepared, are the most powerful tools an expert has in deposition.

- **Identifying the Deposition Attorney's Particular Style**

Every attorney that deposes you will have their own particular style and personality type. If you can identify this at the beginning of the deposition, you are less likely to be taken by surprise.

With experience, I have come to recognize right away the personality and style of the deposing attorney.

There are those who are overtly aggressive, and sometimes even obnoxious. They will try to demonstrate their authority by getting under your skin, rattling you, and making you lose control. They are hoping to get you to say things you don't necessarily mean—which you want to avoid at all costs.

Then, there is the friendly, nice-guy type. This kind of guy makes you feel like he is your best friend, despite the fact that you are meeting for the first time. They will plod along, providing a nice, relaxed pace and atmosphere for you. They are hoping that if you start feeling comfortable enough, you will drop your guard—and they can drop the hammer on you, quickly and deliberately.

Ultimately, as long as you are courteous and confident, and you stick to the facts that support your opinions and conclusion, it makes no difference what kind of attorney you are facing. Being honest, straightforward, and professional will serve you, your client, and your case, very well.

And, even if you do run into that rare exception—a truly obnoxious attorney—it is important to remember that no good can come of arguing, or expressing anger, towards the deposing counsel. It will only reflect badly on you when portions of your deposition are later read aloud in court.

Law 9/48

Law 22/48

- **Maintaining Your Cool in the Face of Intimidation Tactics**

When you take the stand, you are sitting next to a judge—a figure of authority. The atmosphere is formal. The procedures are formal. The interrogation, examination, and deposition processes are formal—and designed to be intimidating!

Every expert—even if they are at the top of their field—feels somewhat intimidated at one time or another. It is only natural. In fact, if you walk into a courtroom and you *don't* feel a little bit anxious and somewhat intimidated, you are feeling too cocky, and it could work against you.

It's not the feeling of intimidation that's the issue. It's how you react to it that makes the difference. The last thing you want to do in deposition or open court is appear to be easily offended, insulted, or taken aback. In order to thrive as an expert witness, you will need to develop some coping skills.

Knowing what to expect is one of the most powerful things you can do to maintain your balance—and your cool. If you walk in *expecting* the process to be an attack on your credibility, honesty, and integrity, you are less likely to be thrown for a loop when it happens.

If, on the other hand, you are taken aback, and react negatively to attacks designed to make you feel inadequate or inferior, you will have a very hard time as an expert witness.

Take these things in stride. Don't overreact. As long as you are respectful and truthful, and answer the questions in a straightforward manner, you're safe.

Opposing counsel can insult and intimidate you all day long, but they won't gain any ground.

- **Trusting Retaining Counsel When Your Back is Against the Wall**

Early in my expert witness career, I was being deposed on a case. The deposing counsel asked me a question. I gave it some thought, and then answered the question.

He asked me the question again. It was phrased in a slightly different manner this time, but it was essentially the same question.

Again, I provided a clear and concise answer. This process went on for four more questions—all basically the same. I answered them accordingly, with the same answer each time.

"Sir!" he said. "You are not answering the question!" He then turned towards retaining counsel and said, "Instruct your expert to answer the question, or not to answer the question."

Retaining counsel turned to me and said, "Mr. Gulya, please answer the question to the best of your ability."

Opposing counsel proceeded to ask me the question two more times—rephrased only slightly each time. And, I provided the same answer as I did each of the four previous times.

The deposing attorney turned red in the face, stood up, pointed at me from across the table, and declared,

"You are being evasive, and refusing to answer the question, despite your counsel's instruction to do so!"

I said, "I have answered your question six times! I cannot help it if you do not like the answer, or if it is not the answer you'd like to hear."

He said, "I'm calling the judge right now to hold you in contempt, or force you to answer! Do you want to hear the definition of contempt?"

He then read to me the following definition: "A court trial hearing or other court proceeding such as a deposition declares a person to have disobeyed or been disrespectful to the court's authority. Such a person can be held in contempt, which is the judge's strongest power to impose sanctions for acts which disrupt the court's normal process."

He was saying to me, in so many words, "You are about to get in big trouble here!" And with that, he whipped out his cell phone, and called the judge.

As all of this was unfolding, retaining counsel was sitting there, quiet as a church mouse, completely devoid of facial expressions. His demeanor gave me no indication as to how much trouble I might or might not be facing.

All I knew was that I had answered the attorney's questions to the best of my ability—and told the truth. What was I supposed to do? Change my answer because it wasn't what deposing counsel wanted to hear?

Nevertheless, opposing counsel's call to the judge took me off guard, and I was nervous. I wondered, *Could I really be in trouble here, even though I answered truthfully?*

I decided not to worry about it. The odds seemed slim that the attorney would actually get the judge on the phone, right then and there, anyway. I figured it would all get sorted out later.

Imagine my surprise when he did get the judge on the phone! Now, I really was a bit nervous. I still didn't necessarily think I had *reason* to be nervous, but knowing the judge was on the phone had me on edge.

The attorney told the judge he had an uncooperative witness who was refusing to answer a question, despite legal counsel's instruction to do so. He then told the judge he wanted to hold me in contempt—or, at the very least, instruct me to answer the question or suffer the consequences of being held in contempt of court.

At that point, the attorney handed the phone to the court reporter. Obviously, I could not hear what the judge had said to opposing counsel, but he must have asked to speak to the court reporter.

The court reporter then began reading from the transcript. When she was done, she handed the phone back to opposing counsel—who handed the phone to retaining counsel.

Within twenty seconds of that, retaining counsel hung up the phone and handed it back to opposing counsel. I didn't know what was being said, and neither did anyone else. We were all on pins and needles, watching and listening.

Opposing counsel advised the court reporter that we were now back on the record. And, with that, he resumed the deposition with an entirely new question.

Finally, retaining counsel spoke up, saying, in essence, "For the record, opposing counsel asked for the judge's ruling regarding the answer our expert, William Gulya, provided *no less than six times*. He asked the judge to hold Mr. Gulya in contempt and force him to answer. The judge ruled that Mr. Gulya answered the question completely and properly, and acted professionally, and just because opposing counsel either did not like the answer he got, or did not get the answer he was looking for, there is no basis for contempt, and no basis to force the witness to provide a different answer."

What he said was entered into the record.

This story illustrates just how forceful some attorneys can be, and how heavily they can lean on an expert, in order to get an answer they want to hear. Talk about intimidation tactics!

Today, I would not be nearly as concerned about the attorney calling the judge, but, at the time, it was quite an intense experience.

You may one day find yourself in a similar position. I can't make any blanket statements about how you should handle such a situation, because your circumstances will be unique. All I can do is share what I learned.

First of all, I learned how imperative it is to remain calm in those types of intense situations. Maintain your professional demeanor—which isn't easy under that kind of pressure!

I learned the most important lesson from retaining counsel's reaction to the debacle. As the experience was happening, I kept thinking, *I'm getting hammered here! I've answered this guy's question I don't know how many times, and I can't answer it any better. Why isn't my attorney jumping up and down, saying, "Asked and answered," or showing some kind of appropriate reaction?*

My attorney was unfazed, even when opposing counsel reached the point where he said, "I'm calling the judge!"

In my mind, the retaining attorney should have piped up in that moment and said, "Wait a minute, Counselor. No need to overreact! Let's talk about this." Instead, he did nothing, and I didn't understand his reasoning.

At the same time, my instincts told me that there must be good reason he was remaining so calm. Then it dawned on me—*there was nothing to react to.* The retaining attorney did not need to prevent the situation from unfolding, because he knew that the opposing attorney was digging his own grave. All he had to do was sit back and let it happen.

Opposing counsel's threat to have the judge hold me in contempt was baseless. The judge wasn't going to force me to change my answer simply because it wasn't what opposing counsel wanted to hear. By calling the judge, the attorney painted himself into a corner.

The retaining attorney was unconcerned with the deposing attorney's threat—and once the threat materialized, the retaining attorney was unconcerned with what the outcome would be.

I learned from this experience that, sometimes, restraining yourself from speaking or reacting can be more powerful than anything you could say or do.

Law 20
48

Law 22

• Refusing to Limit Your Opinions and Conclusions

Towards the end of a deposition, attorneys will often spring a trap along these lines: "Tell me, have you stated all of your opinions in this deposition that you intend to testify to in court?"

It sounds like an innocent enough question, but it is not.

Let me explain. In the vast majority of cases, a deposition is the only opportunity the opposing counsel will have to question an expert witness and hear their response. (Of course, the attorney will have an opportunity to question you in court, but the deposition is in *preparation* for the courtroom questioning.)

In certain instances, the attorney will have to abide by a court-ordered time limit for deposing the expert. So, whether the court has mandated a limited number of hours during which opposing counsel can depose you, or mandated that counsel must depose you on a certain day, this is the attorney's one shot at you.

Given those constraints, the attorney will want to make sure he asks you every question possible before the clock runs down.

Here's the way it is likely to play out: Let's say the attorney has a twelve-hour day in which to depose you. You arrive at the conference room, have a cup of coffee, and start the deposition. After only five questions, the attorney decides he is finished with you.

He then says, "Okay, I believe I have asked you everything I want to. I have only one last question. During this deposition, have you stated all of your opinions you plan to testify to in court regarding this case?"

If you were to say yes, you could be limiting your *future courtroom testimony* to the five questions he asked you during deposition!

Guess what would happen the very first time you were asked a question in court that fell outside the scope of what the opposing counsel asked you in deposition? Before you could even get your opinion out of your mouth, the opposing counsel would speak up, saying, "I object, Your Honor! In his oral deposition, this witness said that his only opinions were confined to the five answers to questions he was asked during deposition."

During a deposition for a case on which I had been hired to opine, I was asked by opposing counsel, "Mr. Gulya, during this deposition, have you stated all of your opinions regarding this case?"

Just because the attorney didn't ask me a question related to a fact or circumstance surrounding the case, it didn't mean I didn't have an opinion on that fact or circumstance. I may very well have had other opinions, but it was not my place to volunteer them, if questions related to them were not asked of me.

So, I gave the following answer: "Counselor, we have been here for three days now. I have stated all I can think of at this point, and have responded to all your questions."

The attorney's tone instantly changed, and he became somewhat irate. He then insisted that I state all my opinions, given that he would not have another opportunity to question me.

This particular case was very complex, involving hundreds of thousands of pages of evidence—

including my own lengthy report, and my lengthy rebuttals of three reports from opposition experts.

After three days of deposition, I did not remember every single question he had asked me related to the voluminous evidence, or every single response I gave him. So, I replied, "Counselor, if you have more questions, I will be more than happy to answer them."

You will notice that, technically, I did respond to the attorney's question—but I did so without saying, yes, no, or even maybe. By choosing to answer as I did, I reserved my right to offer opinions at trial that fell beyond the scope of what I had testified to during deposition.

• Refusing to be Rushed or Put on the Spot

An attorney may also ask you, "Is there any testimony you want to correct at this time?" This is another trap.

This is the way I have answered such a question when it was posed to me: "Counselor, I will be more than happy to read the transcript when it becomes available. I will not be rushed or hurried, or waste the time of the court reporter and everyone else, to have three days worth of transcripts read back to me now."

Did it make sense to have the court reporter read back to me three days of transcripts? No. Was it appropriate to point this out to deposing counsel? Yes.

So, I let the attorney know I would read the transcript when it became available, and if modifications of my testimony needed to be made, I would do so at that time.

At that point, the attorney ended his examination of me, saying, "I have no further questions."

These are examples of the kinds of answers you might want to use, when appropriate. These types of answers allow you to answer questions without getting trapped into responding the way the opposition would like.

The examples I have given here are honest, accurate, and justified replies. In each case, I neither agreed nor disagreed, one way or another; the questions did not justify a yes or no response. They justified a polite and honest reply.

~ 8 ~
TESTIMONY—PART TWO
Courtroom

"When in doubt, tell the truth."
~Mark Twain

Law 28/48
Boldness

• Making a Good First Impression

Every day, we are communicating in both verbal and nonverbal ways. Nowhere is this more true than in the life of an expert witness. Your very ability to be taken seriously depends upon your nonverbal communication. If you don't get that right, all the effort and energy you put into your written and verbal communication will go out the window.

That is the first thing to understand about courtroom testimony—it actually begins the minute you walk into the courtroom. Before you ever open your mouth, you are making a statement that can carry as much weight as anything that comes out of your mouth.

If your appearance is sloppy or unprofessional, it may not matter what you say. The judge and/or jury will hear what your appearance is saying. So, remember, wear professional attire and avoid flashy jewelry.

The same holds true of your demeanor. If you come across as hostile, angry, or reactive, that will speak volumes. Hold your head up as you walk. Be careful not to shuffle your feet. Appear confident—but never arrogant.

When the attorney asks you a question, don't let your eyes wander around the room; make eye contact with the attorney asking you the question. Otherwise, you will give the impression that you are nervous, searching for the answers, or have something to hide. When you are trying to emphasize a point, look directly at the jury. Your goal is to show them that what you are saying is important. And, pay special attention to those who are leaning forward in their seats; those are often the ones who are most interested in what you are saying.

You also want to notice those who appear less interested in your testimony. They may be looking down, leaning back, leaning left or right, or resting their head on one hand. Your goal is to get them interested and convinced that what you have to say is important to the case, and to their decision.

- **Giving Your Testimony—in Court**

  - **Direct Examination**

Direct examination is the questioning of a witness by retaining counsel—the party that called him or her

130

as a witness at trial. During direct examination, the counselors attempt to provide evidence which supports and proves their case.

Since direct examination is the part of the process where you are being questioned by the side that retained you, this is the most comfortable you will ever feel at trial. There will be no compound questions, no trick or trap questions, and no attacks on your credibility.

This is not the attorney who wants to tear you apart. This is the one who wants to make you look as good as possible, and make the evidence look as credible as possible. So, he is going to expound on your qualifications, and on the evidence in your report that supports his client's position.

Interestingly, jurors pay less attention to expert testimony given under direct examination because they know that the retaining attorney is the one doing direct examination, and they are always going to present their best case. It's not that jurors don't listen to, or appreciate, testimony under direct examination— but they don't initially give it a lot of weight.

• Cross-Examination

By definition, cross-examination is the interrogation by opposing counsel of a witness called at trial. Jurors tend to pay more attention during cross-examination, in order to determine whether an expert is truthful and believable. It is widely believed that more cases are lost on cross-examination than during direct examination.

This is where attacks on an expert witness's credibility are going to occur. It is also where the expert's opinions and conclusion will be questioned—along with the facts, and supporting evidence, upon which they were based. It is important not to argue with opposing counsel, and to remember the three P's—poise, professionalism, and persuasiveness.

It is during cross-examination that you will need to be aware of compound questions and traps laid by opposing counsel. This is the time when you will need to call on all of your skills, knowledge, and understanding of human nature and psychology. This is when all of those elements need to come together.

Frequently, retaining counsel and witnesses—be they fact or expert witnesses—will have a mock trial in advance of the trial date. During the mock trial, the retaining attorney will not coach you on what to say at trial, but he will be preparing you for the type of questions and interrogation you can expect from opposing counsel during cross-examination. This gives retaining counsel the opportunity to see how you are going to react under pressure.

It is during cross-examination that it is most critical for you to keep in mind many of the things we've already covered:

Look the examining attorney in the eye when he is asking—and you're answering—questions;

Don't look around the room or shift in your seat. This does not come across well, and may leave the jury with the feeling that you are unsure of yourself.

When you need to emphasize a particular answer you are providing, look away from the attorney, and focus on the jury for a moment. Remember—they are the people you need to educate as to what your answers mean, so don't hesitate to speak directly to them. This shows honesty and conviction in your answers.

It is also important to resist the impulse to look at retaining counsel when you are being examined by opposing counsel. If you start looking towards retaining counsel too often, it gives the jury the impression that you lack confidence in what you are saying. It tells them that the question is troubling to you in some way, and you're looking for the answer, looking for instructions as to what to do next, or waiting for retaining counsel to object, or otherwise get you out of a tight spot.

I have developed a strategy for handling questions that I feel should be—but aren't—objected to by retaining counsel: I simply pause for a few seconds. That tiny pause manages to accomplish a couple of important things.

First, it allows both you and retaining counsel to evaluate the question, which might result in retaining counsel objecting, after all.

If no objection is forthcoming, you can then ask opposing counsel to repeat the question. This provides a few additional seconds to gather your thoughts, and formulate an honest and knowledgeable response.

It also provides retaining counsel a few more seconds, and one last opportunity to reconsider objecting. If retaining counsel *still* does not object to the question, just answer it truthfully and confidently, to the best of your ability.

I am always cognizant of the fact that, even if a question is troublesome, set up to trap me, or can't be clearly answered as presented, clarification can always be accomplished through redirect testimony. So, I don't worry or make a big deal over it.

And, remember, attorneys may cross-examine witnesses for a living, but they will never know as much about your field of expertise as you do. It is your knowledge of your field that will allow the truth, and the facts, to come out. This is the advantage you have over opposing counsel. All the attorney has on his side is his ability to trap you or make you lose your cool.

You will feel more at ease and confident if you can go into a deposition or trial believing that you have the advantage, by virtue of being the one with greater familiarity of your field than opposing counsel.

• Redirect Examination

Redirect examination is conducted by retaining counsel. The term generally applies to trials, but there is a form of redirect that occurs in depositions, as well. In the deposition context, it is not called redirect, but the process is the same.

This is where retaining counsel has the opportunity to clear up any confusion or misconceptions that may have arisen during cross-examination. In depositions, it is also the time when every attorney present gets a chance to ask you questions.

Thanks to redirect examination, no expert ever needs to be unduly nervous or anxious over uncomfortable blunders they may make during cross-examination. A courtroom examination may seem like a slow and arduous process, but things can happen pretty quickly, especially during cross-examination. That is the beauty of redirect examination—it is an opportunity to do some course-correction, and get back on track.

Maybe you didn't express yourself as clearly as you would have liked. Maybe opposing counsel cut you off, mid-sentence. Perhaps you were asked a compound question that you failed to recognize as such. Those things are bound to happen to every expert at some point in time.

There are a couple of drawbacks to redirect examination: The attorney is not allowed to ask new questions; he is only allowed to address your testimony given during cross-examination. So, the witness cannot use this opportunity to present new information, based on new questions or subject matter not addressed during cross-examination.

The other downside: Whenever there is redirect examination, the opposing counsel is again given an opportunity to cross-examine you, as well. Of course, opposing counsel is also limited to those questions that were addressed during redirect examination.

Once I fully understood the redirect process and its purpose, two things happened. First, it made me more comfortable during the potentially grueling cross-examination process, because I understood that I would always have an opportunity during redirect to amend anything I hadn't expressed the way I intended the first time.

And secondly, by making me less nervous, it made me less likely to misspeak, make a blunder, or say something far removed from what I intended in the first place.

It's like knowing you have a parachute—and a spare—when you are jumping out of a plane. Sure, you might be nervous making the jump, but you know you are covered. You have a safety valve. You have backup.

One important note: Even though redirect examination is your opportunity to clear up any misconceptions created during cross-examination, you never want to give the jury the impression that you are chomping at the bit to do so.

The jury might see you as backpedaling, if you come across with the message, "Boy, I'm so glad we had a chance to clear that up!"

This may seem counter-intuitive. In daily life, a person's desire to address—and clear up—a problem is viewed as a good quality. In this arena, it can have the exact opposite effect.

Simply approach redirect in the same way you would approach direct or cross-examination. Be clear, concise, and professional.

• Handling Compound Questions

Attorneys are not necessarily looking for the "correct" answer. They are looking for an answer that favors their case and their client—and they have strategies for asking questions that will elicit just such an answer. Most of the time, this is accomplished through compound questions, which can be tricky. Experts need to quickly recognize and break down compound questions, addressing each question within the question, separately and distinctly.

Keep in mind that, while it is permissible to write down the separate facets of the question on a pad of paper, or to have your report handy for review, it is inadvisable. Testimony should always seem spontaneous and seamless. If you appear to need to reflect back on your report or supporting data, it gives the impression you're not really prepared, or may not understand the facts of the case.

The one exception would be when you have a series of rules, regulations, statutes, or other complex data that you would not be expected to remember, verbatim. Then, and only then, is it appropriate, and advisable, to ask either the court or the opposing attorney for the material in question. In that case, you want to emphasize the fact that you are requesting the material because the data is complex, and you want to be sure you quote it verbatim.

That way, you show that you do know what you're talking about—you just don't have the complex data memorized, verbatim.

If you ever have to request such data or material, read it promptly and thoroughly, so you can accurately answer the question.

Law 29/48

• Standing Your Ground

During deposition, the opposing attorney will have been on the lookout for grounds for impeachment he could try to use against you at trial. (Used in this context, impeachment does not have the same meaning as it does when applied to the ouster of a president. In this context, to impeach the expert is to discredit him.)

During trial, the opposing attorney may read an answer you provided in deposition, and then follow up with a question like, "Tell me, Mr. Smith, do you still stand by that answer?"

When an attorney asks that particular type of question, it's always a red flag for me. When I hear such a question, there is only one question going through my mind: *Has there been new evidence introduced that may necessitate changing my opinion?*

If I am not aware of any new evidence, I stick to my guns, and reinforce my opinion.

The opposing attorney, on the other hand, may know of evidence of which I am unaware, and say to me, "Well, Mr. Gulya, what about this piece of evidence? I do not see it listed in your report."

In that case, I simply reply, "I am unaware of that evidence and have not received it. Without having seen the evidence, I would have to read and evaluate it before I could answer your question."

One time during a deposition, I was asked, "Sir, are there facts or circumstances that might change or alter your opinion in this case?"

I responded as follows: "Counselor, that question is too broad. I could not speculate on every possible scenario. I only evaluated the available evidence in this particular case."

Beware of questions like this, which are framed as broad brush strokes. Stick to the facts and the evidence of the case. Do not speculate.

~ 9 ~

NOTEWORTHY CASES

*"Any fact is better established
by two or three good testimonies
than by a thousand arguments."*
~Marie Dressler

- **A Lesson in Recognizing Clear and Obvious Evidence**

This case involved a piece of property in Utah, upon which a developer was building a medical office complex—which happened to be right next to a major hospital. At the center of the case was a process known as micro-tunneling, which involves drilling a hole, and pumping concrete into it. This is generally done to support, or underpin, the concrete footings upon which a building sits.

In the process of performing this micro-tunneling work, the workers unwittingly drilled into a main sanitary sewer pipe, and began pumping concrete into it. It so happened that this main sanitary sewer pipe was the main discharge pipe for the hospital. As a result, the hospital's sewage backed up, and caused extensive damage to the hospital.

The hospital sued everyone involved—the developer, the general contractor, and the subcontractor. (I was retained by counsel for the developer.) The contention was that the developer was responsible, because he hired the general contractor, who hired the subcontractor, and so on.

There is a very detailed set of specifications or rules that must be followed when micro-tunneling is performed. Without getting technical, one aspect of those rules involves measuring the amount of concrete pumped into the hole that is being drilled.

While those rules and specifications are fairly detailed and complicated, it boils down to one thing—you cannot put two pounds of dirt into a one-pound bag!

That is essentially what happened in this case. The workers completely disregarded the rules—and common sense, for that matter—continuing to fill the hole, until at last somebody spoke up and said, "It seems like we are putting an awful lot of concrete in here!"

Before the hole was drilled and filled with concrete, a number of circumstances were in play. First, there was the "Call before you dig" issue.

A contractor beginning work is obligated by contract, by responsibility, and by drawing specs, to locate all the existing underground pipes before beginning micro-tunneling. Such pipes belong to one or more of the utilities—the phone company, gas company, cable company, water company, and so on.

Most states and regions have a Notification of Excavation phone number—or "Call before you dig" number. Any contractor who is performing excavation or digging needs to call that number, and notify the agency as to where, why, and how they are planning to dig, as well as how deep they are planning to go.

There are a whole host of questions that go along with that process. Once the questions are answered, the appropriate utility companies then go out and mark the boundaries of where their pipes are located, using paint and plastic flags.

If you *don't* call, and you break something belonging to one of those utilities, it is your problem. If you *do* call and you break something, it is still your problem—unless the location where you broke something falls outside of marked boundaries, in which case you might be off the hook.

Let's say the utility company marked their boundaries in a particular location, and the rule of that particular state's excavation notification agency is that a contractor needs to find the utility pipe within three feet of the center line of the location marked. If you happen to break it *twelve* feet outside that center line, you may not be held responsible for the cost to repair it. But, if you break it within the parameters of that state agency's rules, you are responsible. It's that simple.

In this case, the subcontractor did call, and boundaries were marked. In fact, the boundaries were made even more obvious by the presence of cleanouts and pipes, which were sticking up above ground (in case there was a clog and they needed to put down a plumbing snake.)

The problem was, the subcontractor did exploratory excavation, but failed to go far enough to actually *find* the pipe they ended up drilling through and filling with concrete.

Here's what happened: During the exploratory excavation to locate the main pipe, the subcontractor's crew uncovered the cleanout, which went down approximately two feet—a fact they discovered by sticking a shovel handle inside the cleanout. Because the handle only went down a couple of feet, they mistakenly concluded, "This is going way over in that direction, and we are going over here, so this doesn't concern us."

What they did not realize was that, although the cleanout went straight down approximately two feet, *it then turned on a forty-five-degree angle*, continuing down to where the main pipe was located.

They never bothered to find the actual pipe! If they had, they would have discovered that it made a different kind of turn. Instead, they drilled through, and filled it with concrete, causing extensive damage to the hospital.

The conclusion in my report read (in part) as follows: "It is my expert opinion, to within a reasonable degree of certainty, that the developer followed all appropriate protocols…"

To summarize, I concluded that the prosecution could blame the developer all they wanted to, but the developer had done everything he would have been reasonably expected to do. I went on say what went wrong from the standpoint of the general contractor and their subcontractor, and why.

I also stated that, because I am not an attorney, I could not opine on the legalities of the relationship between the developer and the general contractor he hired. I could only opine on what a developer would reasonably and professionally be expected to do, and what the general contractor and their micro-tunneling subcontractor did or failed to do, considering best practices and industry standards.

Ultimately, the developer was released from the case. I also happen to know that this case settled before going to trial—but that is all I know. It is unusual for me to be privy to the detailed outcome of cases, other than being told that a case has settled. In the cases that do go to trial, I may be told the outcome or the verdict, but I'm not generally apprised of the details of the judgment.

The reason for this is pretty simple—the fact that there is a judgment does not necessarily mean there will not be an appeal. For example, if a verdict is issued by the lower court, to the effect that "Party A owes Party B ten thousand dollars," and Party A disagrees with that verdict, they can make the decision to appeal.

In most states, Party A would then be required to do one of two things: Put up one-and-a-half times the verdict value in a cash bond, to be held by the state or federal court, or provide a surety bond to cover the amount of the judgment. (It is important to note that these rules vary by state.)

Thanks to the appeal process, I may never know the ultimate verdict on appeal. It is very, very rare for an expert to be called in on an appellate proceeding, for the simple reason that, by the time the case is being heard before an appeals court, their report and testimony are already part of the record.

• Lessons Learned

Here was a case where you had a developer who apparently did all the right things, and got blamed anyway. He had to go out and hire an attorney, who had to hire an expert. I then had to prove or support the position that the developer did not determine where to drill the hole, or pour the concrete. He did not even hire the subcontractor who did.

He was no expert in the proper methods of performing micro-tunneling or exploratory excavation. He was just the developer, dependent upon the professional expertise of others.

When all was said and done, it was clear that the developer had no control over the subcontractor's actions, or responsibility for the property damage to the hospital.

The Lesson? Don't discount the obvious! Sometimes the truth really is *just that simple*.

The evidence I found was compelling and abundantly clear—the micro-tunneling contractor did not properly locate the existing underground utility pipes, or measure the concrete he was pumping. He did not follow the required specification procedures, best practices, or industry standards, and did not do what was required of him. Instead, he relied upon assumptions.

When I discovered those two red flags—the subcontractor's failure to locate the actual underground pipe, and to measure the amount of concrete he was pumping—I thought, *This is pretty clear! The subcontractor did not perform as he was supposed to. He didn't do what he should have done.*

In the back of my mind, however, nothing is ever that simple. So, I was looking for something that might contradict what I had already found.

That's exactly what an expert should do! Even though the answer *seemed* obvious, I had the obligation to look for clear and compelling evidence of fault or deficiency, wherever it may be found.

It just so happened that in this particular case, the truth really was as simple as it seemed. Most cases are not as clear-cut.

• A Lesson in Seeking Out the Truth

I once had a mysterious case in which I was retained on behalf of a contractor—the defendant. At issue was the fact that the contractor had been putting a water main in a road, and the installation required a valve and valve box. The valve was a standard type, with a cover (a valve box) over the top of it.

The valve in this case was five feet underground. Typically, one would install it in such a way that, ultimately, the top of the valve box was equal to the finished elevation of the road in that particular area.

After the valve and valve box were installed, and the trench was backfilled and compacted, you would put in the base course/binder course—a type of asphalt with bigger stone in it (technically referred to as an I-2 mix), and then a surface course mix (technically referred to as an I-5 mix). The specifications would determine the thickness of each course —for example, six inches of the I-2 mix and two inches of the I-5 surface course mix.

So, the contractor put in the valve and valve box. Then they backfilled and compacted the earth. Now, they were at an elevation where they were putting in their six inches of I-2 asphalt.

Since the finished elevation would end up being two inches higher, the valve box was going to be sticking up two inches.

So, you would typically create a bevel or slope (sometimes also referred to as a ramp or ring) around the valve box. You'd come out anywhere from two to four feet, depending upon the width of your trench, and put in the I-2 or I-5 asphalt. Then, you'd ramp in a circular fashion from the center of the value box, by drawing a circle two feet in diameter around it, and beveling from zero to the top of that valve box.

This is done with manholes, so you have probably seen the finished product a thousand times. The ramping, beveling, and sloping you see around a valve box is a safety measure, intended to prevent a car or truck from hitting an abrupt, sharp metal edge.

While the contractor's crew was working, there was a uniformed traffic officer on duty at the job site. This is normally a requirement on any public street. In addition to the uniformed traffic officer being present, proper traffic cones and construction signs had been put up by the contractor's crew during the construction—which is also a requirement at any job site on a public street.

The contractor's crew finished their work—they installed the valve and valve box, backfilled the dirt, put in the I-2 asphalt mix, and did the sloping/beveling around the valve box. When the end of the workday came, and the crew was ready to go home, it was time to reopen the road to normal traffic.

So, the officer inspected the road to determine whether it was, in fact, suitable to be reopened to public traffic until the following day when the work crew returned. After inspection, the officer reopened the lane that was closed during construction, and the orange safety cones were removed.

Here is where things get interesting. Sometime during the night, or in the early morning hours before the construction crew returned to the job site, a woman was traveling along in her car, and hit the valve box. She sustained injuries, and did extensive damage to her car.

The driver claimed that the valve box was sticking eighteen to twenty-four inches out of the ground!

Now, this is the very same valve box we have been talking about all along. And, as you'll recall, the top of the valve box was equal to the finished elevation of the road. So, how could it be that it was now sticking eighteen to twenty-four inches out of the ground, and above the existing road surface?

During our initial interview, after the retaining attorney explained all of this to me, all I could say was, "This is a mystery! I don't understand how a valve box could magically rise out of the ground like Jack's beanstalk. It is simply not possible!"

And yet, that's exactly what seemed to have happened.

The attorney retained me as an expert witness on the case, and sent me the evidence—what little there was to send. In many cases, I am sent voluminous amounts of evidence. In this case, there were only a few depositions, and a handful of letters back and forth between the various parties. There was nothing an expert would necessarily be able to sink their teeth into.

After reviewing the evidence, I found nothing remarkable—or clarifying. The mystery remained the same.

I started with the things I knew for sure:

One—the fact that valve boxes don't rise magically out of the ground; and

Two—the fact that the traffic officer approved the reopening of the road—which he would not have done had the valve box been sticking eighteen to twenty-four inches out of the ground.

Then I began to ponder the following questions:

Could the contractor on the job site, and the uniformed traffic officer, have both failed in their duties and responsibilities, and allowed the reopening of a road that should not have been opened?

Was everyone in such a hurry to get home for the day that no one noticed that the valve box was sticking up from the ground, a foot-and-a-half to two feet? It seemed incomprehensible that both the traffic officer and the contractor could have failed to notice such a thing—and yet it was remotely possible.

In the absence of any other evidence, what other conclusion could I draw? While it seemed unlikely, it was feasible that both the traffic officer and the contractor's crew were incompetent, and potentially lying to avoid culpability and liability.

The jury might have accepted such a scenario as true and believable. I could have simply left it at that, and let the attorneys argue the competence or incompetence of the contractor and traffic officer—but I didn't.

Something about the whole mystery would not let me rest. I revisited the little bit of evidence I was given, and pored over it with a fine-tooth comb. In so doing, I noticed one small notation, to the effect that the road in question was being utilized by a rather large towing company. A light bulb went on in my head. I had a theory.

In order to prove my theory, I was going to have to do some detective work. So, I went out to the road in question, and stood there. I watched as tow truck after tow truck passed by. I did not see a single tow truck that was not towing a car or truck. As you probably know, when a certain type of tow truck tows a car or truck, the front of the towed vehicle is lifted up, so that the back of the vehicle hangs down, close to the ground.

It all came together in my mind: Imagine that a tow truck is towing a vehicle, which is hanging just a little bit too close to the ground in back. Now imagine what would happen if that tow truck, with the vehicle attached, hit a bump or depression in the road, making the angle of the car even worse, and reducing even further the distance between the bottom of the car and the road.

Now, picture something on the underside or back-side of the vehicle—such as the bumper or rear axle housing—grabbing the lip of the valve box, and yanking it up. Had that happened, the tow truck driver would probably have kept right on going, having no idea what he had done.

Five or ten minutes later, the woman driver in the case happens along, driving down the road. She has the bad luck to be the first person to drive over this valve box since it was yanked up out of the ground. Boom! She hits it, damages her car, and sustains injuries.

Excited that I had finally uncovered a plausible explanation for what happened, I called the retaining attorney. He listened with fascination, and then said something to the effect of, "Well, it looks like you have solved the mystery!"

At the end of the day, it was reasonable to conclude that the valve box was installed properly, according to industry standards and best practices. It was also reasonable to conclude that valve boxes don't rise out of the ground by themselves. And finally, it was reasonable to suggest that it had to have been *pulled out of the ground somehow*—and I had a plausible theory as to how that might have occurred.

Of course, if the case went to trial, opposing counsel could say to me, "But, you didn't personally see this happen, did you?"

And I would have to say, "No, I didn't."

He would have then said to me, "So you are not sure it happened that way, are you?"

To which I would have replied, "No, Sir. However, it is the only reasonable explanation. It could not have risen magically."

The thing is, no matter what the opposing attorney might have said to try to shoot holes in my theory, everyone knows that there are no such thing as magical valve boxes. So, there must be a plausible reason that it was sticking eighteen to twenty-four inches out of the ground.

Unless, of course, you want to take the position that an experienced traffic officer, whose responsibility it was to ensure that the road was in the proper condition to be safely reopened to traffic, is incompetent, untruthful, and completely lacking in credibility.

The case ultimately settled a short time after I submitted my official report. The retaining attorney called to thank me, and tell me I could close my file. Before we hung up, he called me "a modern-day Sherlock Holmes."

I never knew the extent of the driver's injuries, because I was not privy to the medical evidence. But, it appears that, *on the basis of my report alone*, the insurance carrier for the injured driver decided not to take this one to court. The insurance carrier no doubt realized that, in order to say that my theory was wrong, they would have had to come up with a plausible explanation of their own as to *why* I was wrong.

This brings me to the report prepared by the opposition's expert. His first page-and-a-quarter discussed the facts, and his opinions and conclusion related thereto. He started out by listing the documents he had reviewed. This is not my usual approach, but it is effective enough.

His next sentence began with the phrase, "It appears..." He did not present any authoritative information, and instead gave the impression that he was guessing. Experts do not—or should not!—guess. They speak in terms of facts, pure and simple. If it's a fact, it's a fact. If it isn't, it isn't. Using statements like "It appears" sends the wrong message.

As for the content of the opposition's expert's report, he concluded that the incident was caused by the failure of the contractor to properly cone the construction site, and to abide by the recommendations for accident prevention in the AGC Manual for Accident Prevention in Construction.

You will recall that the road was in fact, coned, and had the appropriate traffic signs while they were working. The accident occurred after all of these things were removed, and the road was reopened.

So what did the coning or traffic signs have to do with the accident, itself? Nothing! The opposing expert was grasping at straws.

The opposition's expert's report then went on for six to eight pages, discussing accident prevention regulations, and the Manual on Uniformed Traffic Control Devices. He went into great detail about signage, cones, lights, and how one should impose, or alter, traffic lanes.

None of this was improper, per se. But, despite the fact that he thundered on with copies of all these regulations, throwing in a few nice photos, photocopies, and underlined sections of rules and regulations, his actual report was essentially a-page-and-a-quarter long. And, its focus was on *pre-accident issues* related to safety precautions! It did not address anything that happened after the road was reopened.

None of what he discussed was actually applicable to the case. After all, it wasn't as if, at the hour the accident occurred, there was rerouting of a lane, causing two cars to hit each other; or the rerouting of a lane and a crosswalk, causing a pedestrian to be struck by a car.

The accident occurred in the wee hours of the morning, after the road had been reopened to traffic. Therefore no cones were necessary or required.

• Lessons Learned

The first lesson I derived from this case has to do with the importance of adapting your report to the actual facts and evidence in the case.

Now, I have never met the opposition's expert. I wouldn't know him if one day, we happened to be sitting side by side. I don't know how long he had been practicing as an expert at the time he submitted his report. But, his report definitely raised questions for me:

Did he accept the case *knowing full well* that he did not have anything to offer in support of retaining counsel's position?

Or, did he initially think he could support retaining counsel's position—but, after reviewing the evidence, come to a different conclusion?

What happened at that point? Was he afraid or hesitant to tell the retaining attorney that there was nothing to support the attorney's position? Maybe he decided it was safer to say, "Well, maybe they didn't put up the traffic cones correctly."

Though the expert was only grasping at straws, the attorney may have heard the expert's theory, and seized on it, saying, "Yeah! That's it!"

I can't know for sure what really happened. All I know is that, by focusing on the traffic cones—something that was relevant only before the accident, not during or after—the opposition's expert seemed to hurt, rather than enhance, retaining counsel's case.

If the case had gone to court, his opinion and testimony would have been ineffective, because he could not support the opinions and conclusion he set forth in his report.

The second lesson in this case relates to the analytical dexterity I discussed in Chapter Two. Here was a situation where I had very little evidence before me. And the small amount of evidence I *had* been sent had done little to clarify for me exactly how the valve box could have risen mysteriously out of the ground.

Thanks to my ability to think outside the box (no pun intended!), I was able to recognize in the evidence that tiny detail about the road being used by a towing company. Had I overlooked that one detail, my theory about the tow trucks may have never come to light.

The mystery may have remained unsolved—and the rather implausible theory that both the uniformed traffic officer and the construction crew were derelict in their duties might have been seized upon by attorneys.

Having no other explanation for the accident, they might have had no choice but to argue that theory—potentially calling into question the reputation of both the uniformed traffic officer and the construction crew.

- **A Lesson in Clarifying Your Fee Structure Up Front**

This was a simple property damage case, whereby a private residence was flooded with sewage, to a depth of two to three feet. There was extensive property damage, cleanup costs, and such.

The attorney retained me to opine on whether or not the municipality that owned the main sewer pipes was responsible—and if so, why.

In this particular case, the retaining attorney found me through the website of an expert referral agency. When setting up the initial interview with the attorney, the agency instructed me not to discuss my fee with the inquiring attorney—because they planned to add their fee on top of mine before billing him. This was not unusual for this type of referral agency.

The evidence in this case involved tree roots, old vitrified clay pipe (VCP), and the ancient sewage system in a charming, but older, town in Pennsylvania.

There was a great deal of research to be done, including review of the town sewage authority's maintenance incident reports and complaints, filed by neighborhood residents who experienced the sewers backing up.

Reviewing all those records was necessary in order to prove or disprove responsibility, or even negligence, on the part of the sewage authority.

I performed my duties as an expert witness, and submitted a bill for approximately $8,000.00 to the referral agency. They planned to add their fee, and bill the attorney.

After about three months had passed, and I still had not received payment—which was very unusual—I called the referral agency. I said, "What is going on here, exactly? It has been ninety days and I still have not been paid!'

"Well," they explained, "the attorney has a problem with your invoice, and we need to get it cleared up before we can get you paid."

They proceeded to ask me several questions related to the tasks I had performed as an expert witness on the case. As discussed in an earlier section, I am meticulous about my record-keeping and time-tracking, so I always have a record of what I have done, and how long I spent doing it. Because I kept track of my billable time on this case through specialized software, it was easy for me to supply the information the agency was requesting.

Then they asked me, "Did the attorney ever set a limit on the amount of money she was willing to spend for your expert services?" That question struck me as a little bit odd.

I told them that she had not—which was the absolute truth. Had the attorney ever said that to me, I would have requested to be immediately withdrawn from the case.

Once the referral agency had asked all their questions, and I had answered them, I said, "Please try and work this out with the attorney. I'm sure you can get it straightened out relatively quickly."

So, the referral agency and the retaining attorney talked, and came to a potential settlement agreement. Here's what happened:

My total invoice was $8,000.00—but the retaining attorney would only agree to pay me $3,500.00. The referral agency knew I would never accept that. So, they agreed to add $2,500.00 out of their pocket, which meant I would take an overall cut of $2,000.00.

In effect, the referral agency said they would contribute $2,500.00 toward my final invoice value, and asked me to reduce my overall invoice by $2,000.00.

As part of the settlement agreement, the retaining attorney was proposing that language be included to the effect that, if she ever needed my services in the future, the fee for those services would be paid on "a predetermined, reasonable basis in advance."

Or, in plain language, she wanted me to agree that, if she ever had to come to me and say, "Okay, we need your services for a supplemental report, deposition, or trial testimony," I would charge her a flat fee for whatever amount I expected those services to cost, and get her approval before going over the flat-fee amount I had estimated.

I told the agency, "Listen, I will agree to the $2,000.00 deduction in my fee. However, if she needs my services for this case in the future, she must first agree to pay me the $2,000.00 that is being deducted, as well as any future fees that may be required. In addition, I will only work by the hour, not on a fixed-fee basis. And, my retainer must be paid in full, in advance!"

After telling them what I would agree to, another month went by, and the attorney still had not responded to my counter-offer. I still had not been paid. When the attorney did finally respond, I was advised by the referral agency that she rejected my counter-offer.

At this point, I decided to break with protocol, and called the attorney, myself. When I got her on the line, I asked, "What is going on here in terms of your refusal to pay my invoice?"

Imagine my surprise when she told me that she had an agreement *with the referral agency* not to exceed a certain total billing value! I had no way of knowing whether or not that was a true statement, but the fact that the referral agency was willing to kick in $2,500.00 of their own money to settle the matter made me think there might be truth to what the attorney was saying.

I then proceeded to tell the attorney—using the same perfectly pleasant manner she had been using with me during our call—that I had no intention of agreeing to her settlement offer.

After more time passed with no resolution, I reached the end of my rope. I began corresponding with the referral agency's in-house legal counsel. I quoted several articles from our contractual agreement, and made my position clear, stating, "You need to either get this thing settled or sue the attorney. At this point in time, I don't really care how you get it done. Just get it done!"

I let them know there was no way I was going to agree to the retaining attorney's original offer. I said, "So, you have my permission to take immediate legal action to collect my entire fee, plus costs, unless she's willing to agree that if she needs me again, she will pay me—in advance!—the amount by which she is reducing my fee, plus estimated costs of whatever she is asking me to do in future!"

There was one more issue I needed to clear up with the agency. My contract with them stated that I would be responsible for 40% of any attorneys' fees incurred in the collection of my fee.

"And one last thing," I said. "If it gets to the point where you have to resort to legal action to collect my fee, keep in mind—you made this deal! I did not. So, you are welcome to try to compel me to pay the 40% in legal costs. But, if you try, not only will I refuse to pay it, I will bring a lawsuit against the attorney, myself, *and name you as a party to it!*"

The referral agency knew they had screwed up by agreeing to limit my billable hours, and failing to inform me. I told them as much, flat out.

They communicated to the attorney my position, as follows: There was no way I was going to take a reduction in my fee, and later be asked to represent the attorney again, unless they agreed to pay the reduction I was agreeing to presently, plus future costs, with a retainer paid in advance.

The retaining attorney and the referral agency must have figured that was the best deal they were going to be able to make, because a short time later, my fee was wired into my account. The referral agency must have realized that not paying their expert was bad for business, and the retaining attorney must have realized that not paying their expert would be very embarrassing for them if they ended up in court, in front of their peers and a judge.

At the end of the day, cooler heads prevailed, as they usually do. Everyone saw that they needed to keep the situation from going from bad to worse— and that the only way to do that was to pay my fee.

- **Lessons Learned**

Law 28 *Lions Circle Hesitant Prey*

The first lesson I learned from this situation? Sometimes, you have to take a position of strength, and refuse to veer from that position. I believe that's one of the reasons I ended up getting paid—because I communicated to both the referral agency and the attorney, in no uncertain terms, that I was prepared to do whatever needed to be done to collect my fee.

The second lesson? It is critically important to stay on top of your payment situation, regardless of whether you are dealing directly with a lawyer/law firm, or dealing with a referral agency that has a contract with the lawyer/law firm.

It is easy to become complacent about your payment situation, thinking, *Well, they are contractually obligated to pay me, so I'm sure I'll get paid.*

The reality is, once an attorney has your report, you no longer have anything they need. Or, not in the short term, anyway. And, once you have lost your leverage, they can lose their incentive to pay you in a timely fashion. (Of course, if they don't settle their case, or anything else unforeseen arises, they may very well need your services again. Then the tables could turn.)

What does an attorney have to lose by not paying you, once they no longer need you? After all, attorneys have all the resources they need to defend a non-payment suit filed against them. They live in the legal world, and defending such suits is what they do all day long. But, while it may cost them next to nothing to defend such a dispute, initiating legal action could be quite expensive for you!

The final lesson here: It is important for an expert to remain vigilant about their payment situation, but, when all is said and done, all deals come down to a certain amount of trust.

In the construction business, I do 100% of the work on a job, and get paid 90% percent of the money. The last 10% (a retainage) only gets released upon the final inspection and approvals of engineers, and in accordance with whatever contract governs the job. In effect, I am doing 100% of the work for 90% of my fee!

Now, what if the engineer decided to sit around for a couple of years and not put his stamp of approval on the job? On a million-dollar job, that could amount to the withholding of $100,000.00! But, it would cost me $50,000.00 or $60,000.00 to sue to collect that money.

A contract can always be breached. If you have to enforce a contract, it's not worth the paper it's written on. So, I have to have a certain amount of trust in whatever attorney is retaining me. I have to believe that I will get paid.

I have known experts who have written to a judge, saying, "This attorney owes me $20,000.00, and they are not paying me. Yet, they expect me to come to court and testify. I told them I am not going to testify until they pay me the money they already owe me. They have threatened to sue me for damages to their client's case if I do not testify. I respectfully request that you make a ruling on whether or not it is permissible for me to withdraw from the case."

Then, it's up to the judge. If he rules that you have to show up and testify, regardless of payment issues, you have no choice. Don't fight it, just go to court and do your job to the best of your ability.

It is worth noting that lawyers are aware that an unhappy expert is not a good thing. They are likely to realize that, if you are not paid in a timely fashion, you may not perform at your best—which could hurt their case. This is the last thing they would want. So nonpayment occurrences will be the rare exception, not the rule.

• **A Lesson in Setting Aside the Emotional Component of a Case—Part One**

An emotional case involved a worker named Alberto, who was working with a machine called a hydra-borer, designed to drill horizontally under the ground.

Let's say someone wants to put a conduit or pipe under a driveway, but their driveway is fancy, and they don't want to rip up the driveway or destroy it. Instead, they might opt to drill or horizontally bore beneath it.

The machine works in the following way:

Picture a driveway. You are going to dig a hole on either side of the driveway. On one side of the driveway (referred to as the sending side—the side on which the machine is set up), you are going to dig a trench ten feet in length, and as deep as you want the pipe to be that is going to go under the driveway.

On the opposite side of the driveway (referred to as the receiving side), you are going to dig another trench. This one only has to be a few feet long, and at an equal depth to where the pipe comes out of the other side.

Now, everyone is familiar with the way a drill works, and a hydra-borer is basically a drill—only a whole lot bigger, with drill bits in ten-foot-long sections. Picture a bit on the end of a pipe (the drilling rod) that is about ten feet long. This drilling rod hooks up to a machine and spins very, very rapidly—just like a typical drill would, except, horizontally in this case, rather than vertically.

By their very nature and design, these drilling rods have a certain amount of flex to them, but not to the extent that they can be bent all over the place.

So, this hydra-borer machine was sitting at ground level, and they had a trench that ran ten feet in front of it, and was perhaps two feet deep.

This meant that the drilling rod had to arc (or bend) to where the machine was sitting, and arc (or bend) down to the bottom of the trench. As the drilling rod started penetrating the ground, and drilling horizontally through it, the machine was traveling forward and pushing it along.

Considering the width of this driveway (which in this case we will call twenty-five feet), one ten-foot drilling rod was not going to get the job done. So, the crew had to drill to approximately half the distance of the rod (or five feet), and then back up the machine, attach another rod to the first one, and repeat the process. They were essentially hooking two pieces of pipe together and repeating the process, until they covered the requisite distance under the driveway.

Since the rod was bent, arcing downwards, and spinning very rapidly, something was needed to guide it, in order to keep it going in the right direction, and at the proper elevation or level.

It is important to note that an optional piece of equipment was available for sale— a rod-guiding kit, consisting of guiding anchors for the drilling rods. As I said, these rod-guiding kits are optional, rather than standard equipment, and they are very expensive.

So, what many contractors will do is use very long, heavy pry-rods, or pry-bars. They have the appearance of a six-to-seven-foot-long crowbar. Contractors jab them into the ground, and push them against the spinning drill rod to keep it aligned, pointing in the correct direction, and at the proper depth.

There are warning labels all over the machine, letting the user know, in words and symbols, that under no circumstances should they ever put their foot on these spinning drill rods. Among these warning labels is an entanglement label.

Despite all the labels warning him not to, Alberto decided he was going to use his feet and legs to push the violently spinning drill rod, in an attempt to guide it in one direction or another. Such an action is *extremely dangerous* under any circumstances, but to make matters worse, it just so happened that one of the rods was slightly bent, or flexed. Due to a slight deformity in the rod; it was not perfectly straight. So, it was whipping a little bit more than usual.

Here's why this is significant: If you watched a perfectly straight drill bit in motion, you would not notice it moving, beyond the usual spinning action. But, if you put a *bent* bit in a drill and watched how it whipped around, you would definitely see the difference. Even the slightest bend in a ten-foot drilling rod would exacerbate this whipping effect.

As Alberto used his foot and leg to push down in one direction or the other to guide the rod, it grabbed his pant leg, entangling him in the machine, and causing severe injury to him. Ultimately, he had to have his leg amputated above the knee.

Because of his injuries, Alberto sued, and named many parties in the lawsuit.

Since the project involved installing a cable conduit, so a phone service provider could put their cable under the driveway, the named defendants included the phone company, the general contractor, and everyone involved in the project. Also included was the company that sold the hydra-boring machine to the contractor—the client being represented by the attorney that hired me.

It was alleged that the company that sold the machine to the contractor had a duty to instruct, advise, and follow up on the use of that machine. It was also being alleged that the rod-guiding kit should have been required—not optional—equipment, and that the dealer/seller of the machine, by failing to offer this rod-guiding kit to the buyer, failed in their duty to provide a machine that would operate safely.

Or, in plain words, the allegation was that the seller of the equipment never informed the buyer that the optional rod-guiding kit was even *available*—and even if they had, the kit should have been *required* equipment, rather than optional.

Those were the general allegations of the case. The facts, themselves, were much more complex. There was not one particular fact I could point to and say, "This is why the retaining attorney's client is not responsible for Alberto's injuries."

To sum up my opinions and conclusion: I came to within a reasonable degree of certainty that the dealer/seller of the equipment had fulfilled their obligation to the buyer when they instructed the buyer to read, study, and abide by the professionally developed safety and operating manuals of the machine.

Here is where the emotional aspect of this case comes in: Even though I was not working on behalf of the attorney representing him, I felt terrible about what happened to poor Alberto.

However, *my compassion for Alberto did not change my opinions or conclusion*, which I based upon the following: The operation and safety manuals are developed by the manufacturer of the machine. The manufacturer is the expert in developing those particular manuals, warning labels, etc. The retailer/seller does not develop them.

Additionally, there was no question in my mind that the responsibility to train the contractor's employees on the safe operation of that particular machine, as outlined in and recommended by the safety manuals, fell to the contractor—who failed to do so.

On top of that, Alberto *admitted* that he knew that the warning label meant he should not use his foot to guide the spinning, drilling rod! He also admitted that he knew that there was a known, and perceived, danger to him, if he did.

In summary, many facets of this situation combined to form my opinions and conclusion, but I based my opinions and conclusion primarily upon three things:

One—the seller/dealer fulfilled their obligation by referring the buyer to the manufacturer-developed safety and instruction manuals that were supplied with the machine, which *do* mention and describe in detail the available rod-guiding kit;

Two—the contractor failed to train his people according to those manuals; and

Three—the injured employee, Alberto, failed to use good judgment; he knew he was in danger of being injured if he used his feet to guide the drilling rods, and yet he did so, anyway.

• Lessons Learned

There were two major reasons why the emotional component of this case had a profound effect on me:

First, imagining the pain Alberto had to endure really struck a nerve with me, despite the fact that I had been retained on the opposite side of the case.

I had been retained before on horrific cases where people were run over by pieces of equipment, hit by pieces of equipment, and even buried alive in trench collapses, but none of those cases seemed as disturbing to me as this one. On this particular case, Alberto got injured—and ultimately had to have one of his legs amputated above the knee!—which filled my head with images of his leg being entangled in the drilling rod, and ripped apart.

Secondly, I was deeply troubled by the realization that Alberto could end up receiving no financial compensation whatsoever, because—despite his admittedly severe injuries, and all his pain and suffering—the evidence clearly did not support Alberto's position in the case.

It showed unequivocally that the party on whose behalf I was retained should not have even been included in the lawsuit in the first place. The dealer/seller of the machine had nothing to do with Alberto's injuries, and was in no way responsible for them. They were released from the lawsuit.

I don't know whether Alberto will ever receive any compensation from any of the other parties named to the lawsuit.

There is no doubt that the emotional content of this case was very high. And, there is no doubt that Alberto, the person at the heart of this case, was hurt, and suffered terribly. But, the emotional component of the case does not change the facts, the evidence, or my expert opinions and conclusion.

In the life of every expert witness, there will be times when the evidence simply does not support holding the party or parties to a case responsible for the admittedly horrific damages or injuries suffered or sustained by the plaintiff or defendant in a case.

- ## A Lesson in Setting Aside the Emotional Component of a Case—Part Two

Another case that had a profound impact on me involved an elderly woman who walked directly into, and fell down, an open, five-foot deep trench.

She has since passed away. It is not alleged that she died as a result of this particular incident, although the general feeling is that the incident may have contributed to her death. That, however, is only supposition; it is not being alleged as fact, which is important to understand.

In this particular case, I happened to be have been retained by the plaintiff's side—the attorney of the family of the now deceased woman. The lawsuit was related to injuries the woman sustained from the fall.

The reason this case struck a nerve with me is simple—it involved an elderly lady. I'm not sure I would have been impacted as strongly had it been a younger woman; I happen to have a soft spot for older people, as many do.

So, to continue, I was hired by the decedent's family, who was suing the electric company responsible for digging the trench. The electric company had hired a contractor to do the trenching and install the piping or conduit. The contractor was also named as a party to the lawsuit.

Here's what happened:

The construction company (the contractor) was digging a trench next to a school in one side of a two-lane road. They had left several hundred feet of this trench open, and inside the trench was a pipe they had just installed.

It so happened that a neighborhood event was being held at the school at the same time that the work crew was working on the open trench—during daylight hours.

The granddaughter of the elderly lady was driving her grandmother to the event at the school when she saw construction going on. She noticed some orange cones, spaced at intervals of ten to fifteen feet along the road, but, from her vantage point, it was impossible to tell that there was an open trench.

The parking lot being used for the event was located much further up the road, and the young lady did not want her elderly grandmother to have to walk the distance from the remote parking lot back to the school. So, she suggested that her grandmother get out of the car nearer to the entrance to the event, and walk across to the sidewalk.

Keep in mind, both the granddaughter and her grandmother were totally unaware of the open trench. There was no dirt piled up to indicate a hole—there was just a hole in an asphalt road. And, there was no perspective from which one would necessarily recognize it as a hole, despite the fact that it was broad daylight outside.

So, the grandmother got out of the car, and started walking towards the sidewalk, in the direction of the school. As she walked, she went right in between two of the orange cones set up just inside the center line of the two-lane road. As she was walking between the orange cones, the workers—who were several hundred feet north of her—saw her beginning to walk towards the open trench, and went into a panic.

They began yelling and screaming, trying to get her attention so they could warn her. The problem was, she could not hear or understand *what* they were saying; all she could hear was a loud noise. She looked up in the direction of the noise—while still walking towards her destination.

Boom! Down into the trench she fell. An ambulance came and took her away, and she was treated for her injuries. The details of her injuries were not revealed to me when I was retained to opine on whether or not the contractor had provided the required safety barricades and warning devices to prevent someone from walking into an open trench.

I directed my attention to the manuals for traffic and pedestrian safety. I reviewed the manuals, and all the evidence in the case.   MUTCD

I reached the following conclusion: The contractor had failed to comply with the permit requirements and restrictions which clearly stated, under Title 28 of the NYC/Staten Island administrative codes, "Any person who removes, opens, or otherwise disturbs the pavement or excavates in a public street, or uses any part of that public street to obstruct travel within, must provide barricades, shoring, lighting, warning signs, or other protective measures." The contractor had done none of those things.

There were several additional sections of that code that stated, in effect, that the contractor needed to protect the public from this particular type of danger. They clearly failed to do so.

As part of my final analysis, I had to include the legal definition of negligence, which I did (see the section on Negligence in the last chapter). It was part of my opinion that the contractor was negligent, because the permit restrictions and required actions included a section called Title 12, which held that, "All unattended, open excavated/excavation trenches to be barricaded, or safety railing constructed, to an implied height of not less than forty-two inches."

It was my professional expert opinion that the contractor failed to provide adequate and required safety devices, railings, and signage.

• Lessons Learned

I felt just as badly for the injured grandmother as I felt for Alberto, who lost part of his leg. But in both cases, it was the evidence—not my emotional response to the parties' injuries!—that drove the formation of my opinions and conclusion.

I had one job, and one job only—to analyze the evidence, and form opinions and a conclusion based thereon. I never lost sight of that fact.

It just so happened that analysis of the evidence in Alberto's case *did not* support a conclusion in favor of Alberto, whereas in the case of the elderly lady who fell into the trench, *it did.*

• A Lesson in Dealing With the Unexpected

My company had been contracted to perform earth work, underground piping, and grading of land. Within the scope of that project, we were also contracted to lay down a parking lot, and install curbs and a sidewalk.

The *original* scope of work called for a brick paver crosswalk, for which there was a detail on the contract drawings. The scope of work was changed, however, from a brick paver crosswalk to a red concrete crosswalk, for which there was no detail on the drawings. The revised scope of work listed simply "a red-colored pedestrian concrete crosswalk."

Once the scope of work had been changed, our client, the general contractor, provided only *written* specifications for the new red concrete crosswalk—no drawings.

We proceeded to install the concrete crosswalk, per the written specifications received from our client. After it was completely installed, the owner's engineer rejected our work, citing as his reason, "This is stained concrete! We wanted integral color. The work is hereby rejected. Remove and replace."

This was an $85,000.00 issue for my company!

Let me briefly explain the two different methods by which one could achieve a red-colored sidewalk. Integral color indicates uniform color throughout the concrete. Stained concrete, on the other hand, is achieved by pouring concrete (which is usually grayish white in color), and then sprinkling a powder dye on the top of it, which stains the concrete the desired color, much like wood stain on wood.

When, at the behest of the owner's engineer, the general contractor (our client) rejected our work on the sidewalk, we argued that the written specs we had received did not indicate that they wanted integral color. They had simply asked for a red concrete sidewalk.

Meanwhile, at the job site, a portion of an older building was to be demolished by a company other than mine. Then, the building's basement area was to be backfilled and compacted to a specified grade or elevation (by the demolition contractor). Once that was done, we were to construct a new parking lot on top of what used to be the basement.

During the course of the demolition and backfilling of the basement by the other company, we observed that the contractor's crew performed no compaction.

Now, according to our contract, we were to notify our client in writing if we felt that existing conditions would prevent us from constructing a portion of our work according to industry standards. So, we did. We notified them about what we had observed in regards to the basement compaction issue.

We also requested that they supply soil-compaction tests of the backfilled basement area, to assure us that it had been compacted properly and correctly, per industry standards.

Our client flatly refused, insisting that we proceed with building the parking lot. They offered no reason. They simply said, "No! We are not providing you with any test results. Please install the parking lot as per our contract."

Well, we were not about to install an asphalt parking lot, and then find ourselves responsible if the lot were to sink or fail in some fashion. So, we refused to proceed, telling them why.

Several weeks passed, and the problem remained unresolved. Then, our client, whom I will call Mr. X, requested a meeting, which was to occur at the job site on a particular date. I marked my calendar, and planned to attend the meeting as scheduled.

I believed that it was going to be a private meeting between Mr. X and me. So, you can imagine my surprise when I arrived at the job site, parked my car, and saw several people awaiting me, in addition to Mr. X!

There was the demolition contractor that had knocked down the building and backfilled the basement, Mr. X's project manager and project foreman, the architect's representative, the owner's representative, and the civil engineer's representative.

Clearly, Mr. X must have figured there was strength in numbers. There was no doubt in my mind that he was trying to intimidate me.

I began walking towards the area where everybody was gathered, and as I did so, Mr. X, accompanied by his project manager, walked up to me. When we were finally face to face, Mr. X said to me, "Okay, Bill, what's your f***ing problem???"

As he said this to me, he was a normal talking distance away.

I was completely taken off guard by his opening remark, and said, "I don't have a problem. You do!"

At that point, he got in my face, and said, "This is all your f***ing problem!"

I could see that this meeting was going nowhere. It was not designed to resolve the issue at hand; it was designed to bully and intimidate me.

I decided that it would be best to remove myself. So, I took a couple of steps back from him, turned slightly away, bent down, and started writing on a notepad some notes about who was in attendance at the meeting. I knew I would want to remember those details later. I was not writing down the belligerent comments of Mr. X. There would have been no point in doing so. I merely wanted a general record of the meeting.

As I bent down to write on my notepad, he grabbed my arm with two hands, and flipped me around. I was stunned—and angry!

I am a professional, a businessman, a peace lover. But, when another grown man assaults me, my first instinct is to react. I was about to do just that when Mr. X's project manager jumped between us, preventing an all-out fistfight. Some colorful language was exchanged, and then I regained my wits, and realized I needed to turn and walk away—immediately.

I returned to my office, and got out my camera. First, I took photos of the bruises Mr. X had left on my arm. Then, I called our company's legal counsel, and recalled the day's events to him in detail.

"What can I do, now?" I asked him. "They are expecting us to remove and replace the crosswalk, and install the parking lot, but there is no way I will ever meet with him again. I don't ever want to speak to him again! Also, there is no way I am subjecting my employees to this kind of intimidation! I am afraid there could be more violence."

Our legal counsel instructed me, "They are clearly in breach of contract. He can't just assault you like that! Leave the job site!"

Neither the assault nor the other issues could be resolved, so we took the case to court.

Now, here was a situation where I was both the principal of the company bringing the lawsuit, and an expert witness on behalf of my own company.

As for Mr. X, he also called an expert witness, who testified in court to the language in the contract, as well as policies, procedures, industry-wide compaction standards, etc.

The judge asked me many direct questions. Since this was a bench trial, this wasn't all that unusual. In a bench trial especially, the judge has wide latitude to ask whatever they want. But, the questions were framed in such a way that I felt like the judge was representing the defense. She came across as anything but impartial.

The first issue at the trial: It was my expert opinion that the specs called for colored concrete, but never specified which method they wanted—stained or integral. As such, it was left to the choice or discretion of the contractor (me).

The Judge asked me, "Mr. Gulya, what is the basis of your opinion?"

I said, "It's relatively simple, Your Honor. They did not specify which method they wanted. Therefore, they left it up to the contractor to choose."

She then asked, "Don't you think that the contractor should have asked which one they wanted?"

"But, Your Honor," I replied. "We did ask our client! Here's a copy of the email." (You will note that she is questioning me as if she is opposing counsel.)

The email stated the coloring technique that would be used (a stained coloring technique), and indicated the color number. The color chart that the color number corresponded to was attached to the email. The email also stated that we would provide a mockup sample.

The second issue that was raised at trial had to do with the basement compaction. The judge asked me, "Mr. Gulya, it is your opinion that it was your responsibility by contract to notify your client in writing of any existing condition that would prevent you from otherwise properly installing the parking lot. Is that true?"

I said simply, "Yes, Your Honor, that's true."

She continued, "And, you claim you observed either little or no compaction in this basement area, and you asked for compaction test results."

I said, "That's also true, Your Honor."

The judge then asked, "Where in your contract does it say they must supply you with these particular test results?"

I said, "Well, Your Honor, it is not specified in my contract. However, it is industry standard that any area to be backfilled that will have structural construction on top of it, such as a building or parking lot, must be compacted to 95% or greater. That is the accepted industry and engineering standard."

She replied, "But there is no requirement that they must provide you with those test results in your contract."

I had to admit that there was no specific article in the contract to that effect.

After direct and cross-examination by the attorneys, I was then questioned by the judge concerning the assault. Once again, her manner was such that I felt like she was biased, and representing the opposing side.

"Mr. Gulya," she stated, "it is clear from all the evidence I have seen, that you and Mr. X did not get along."

I said, "That is true, Your Honor. We did not get along. Mr. X was constantly scheming to get work done without compensating my company fairly and properly."

She continued, "So you're alleging, Mr. Gulya, that it was Mr. X that assaulted *you?* I have seen pictures of your arm that are dated and time-stamped that would support that, as well."

I replied, "That is true, Your Honor. That is my testimony."

She then asked, "And, what proof do you have that it was Mr. X that assaulted you, and it wasn't a mutual explosion of temperaments?"

As I said, judges have wide latitude to ask questions, especially during a bench trial. In this case, however, she appeared biased—not because she had taken it upon herself to question me, but because of the particular questions she was asking.

I had shown her pictures of a bruised arm. She was now saying that, for all she knew, it was a simultaneous and mutual altercation that was responsible for my bruises. What could I say?

So, I replied, "All I have is my testimony under oath, which is the truth, the whole truth, and nothing but the truth."

Interestingly, the defense never produced *one witness* that disputed my personal testimony that Mr. X assaulted me. In fact, they never again mentioned the assault after that point in the trial.

The judge ruled that the assault, while an egregious act, was not a basis for breach of contract, because Mr. X and I never had to actually *meet* again in order for my company to complete the project.

Going into court, it seemed highly unlikely that the court would find that Mr. X was not in breach of the contract. Yet, I lost the entire case—the breach of contract argument and everything that went with it.

So, how could this situation have played out this way? Let's look again at the factors that seemed to be in my favor:

Mr. X assaulted me, and produced no witnesses in court to dispute that fact;

I provided my expert opinion as to industry-wide compaction standards of 95%—and there was a complete lack of evidence proving that the demolition contractor compacted to that degree; and

The specs concerning how the concrete was to be colored were completely absent.

Yet, my company ended up having to remove and replace the stained concrete pedestrian sidewalk we had installed. And, we were held responsible for the cost to install the parking lot over the basement. (Because we refused to return to the job site and perform that work ourselves, they had to have it built by someone else.)

By virtue of the court's ruling that our client did not breach his contract, we were held responsible for the difference between the contract value of that parking lot, and the cost to have someone else build it.

Thanks to the court's ruling, when all was said and done, we were out $25,000.00.

• Lessons Learned

What can we learn from this case?

Lesson one—you never know what the outcome of a case is going to be, despite clear evidence showing *unequivocally* that a wrong has been done.

You can not anticipate what a judge or jury is going to think or do, or how they are going to rule—regardless of your expert analysis of the evidence, and your expert opinions and conclusion as to whether or not industry standards or best practices were met, or safety regulations followed.

All you can do is the best, most thorough job possible to convince the judge or jury that your opinions and conclusion are correct. If you do your best, then at the end of the day, you know that, win or lose, you did the most thorough and competent job you could, and there was nothing more you could have done.

And remember, no matter *how* good a job you do, there's no way to know how a judge or jury will rule. This case perfectly illustrates this point. It was clear that an assault took place. Nobody disputes that it was instigated by Mr. X. It was also clear that the specs concerning how the concrete was to be colored were absent. Yet, the judge saw it differently.

Does that mean I did not do a good job as an expert for my own company? Not at all. I based my opinions on factual evidence, and did a thorough job. Still, the judge saw fit to rule in favor of the opposition in this case.

Could my appearance as an expert witness for my own company have impacted the outcome? Possibly. I have always suspected that an expert for his or her own company is viewed as biased, before they ever even step into the courtroom, or speak a word of testimony.

Lesson two—whenever possible, it's a good idea to avoid being named as an expert witness on behalf of your own company.

~ 10 ~
THE STRAIGHT TRUTH

"It is by doubting that we come to investigate,
And by investigating that we recognize the truth."
~ Peter Abelard

- **Withholding Your Report Until You are Paid—the Pros and Cons**

When hired by an attorney, I always receive a retainer in advance, to be applied to the last invoice. In advance of issuing my expert report, I always require that outstanding balances be paid in full. Working with some referral agencies may require an exception, as they handle all billing, payment, and collections.

There is one caveat to all of this: Even though *theoretically* I believe that an expert should never hand over his report until he's been paid, an expert cannot always abide by that principle. Imagine me telling a lawyer/law firm, "You are not getting my report until you pay me in full, even though you need the report tomorrow morning."

That lawyer is likely to say to me, "If you do not give me that report, I will sue you for damages to my case and my client!"

Would the attorney prevail in court, once the judge or jury learned that the attorney was expecting me to perform my end of the contract, without ever performing theirs? It's hard to say.

But, I wouldn't let it go that far, and here's why. One—I don't need that kind of headache. Two—it would ruin my chances of ever again being retained by that particular lawyer/law firm. And, three—I don't need that kind of publicity.

The last thing I want is for an attorney that is considering retaining me to be talking to an attorney that has something negative to say about me.

So, contrary to my personal philosophy that I should never turn in my report before being paid, I have done it in the interests of good faith and the client's case.

I believe that working *with* people, rather than *against* them, is the best road to success. That means that there will be occasions (like the case I described in a previous chapter) where I will be hurt by an attorney refusing to pay my bill.

Those rare occurrences do not justify taking such a hard line that I insist on payment in full before submitting my report. There's no doubt that such a policy may be good practice in theory. In the real world, however, it's not worth the potential adverse effects.

Whenever you can, get paid in full before providing your expert report. However, do not be inflexible.

I am reminded of a case in which my construction company was involved. The case went to arbitration, and the arrangement was such that the arbitrator's fee was to be shared between the parties. It was a simple case, disposed of within a day or two. After the arbitration, I received a notice that the arbitrator had reached a decision—and would be happy to provide his decision *once he was paid in full.*

Isn't this equivalent to an expert demanding his fee before handing over his report? No, it isn't. The difference is threefold.

First of all, the arbitrator was in possession of something both parties needed—the decision or verdict. He was holding all the cards, and so he was able to demand payment before providing his decision.

Secondly, the arbitrator didn't have to worry about alienating potential future clients.

Lastly—and this is perhaps the most salient point of all—by withholding his decision until he got paid, the arbitrator was not causing harm to anyone. The only parties involved were those who had made an agreement among themselves to share the arbitration costs.

An expert witness, on the other hand, is potentially causing harm to someone *outside* of the nonpayment dispute—the client of the attorney. Regardless of how I might feel about an attorney or a law firm that is refusing to pay me, I would never want to jeopardize the case of that attorney's client.

• Dealing with Conflicting Testimony

An expert has to take special care when he encounters conflicting witness testimony in evidence provided to him on a case.

If you have, for example, the depositions of three witnesses whose testimony differs on an important aspect of the case, you can not simply choose the witness that seems most plausible, and side with him. If you do, the opposing counsel will tear you apart.

Here's how it would likely play out: "So, Mr. Expert, we have the testimony of Charlie, Joe, and Sam, and they all say different things—yet you believe Sam. Why?"

You had better have a damned good answer! And you had better be able to back up your answer with evidence and demonstrative evidence.

It is also helpful if you can find another, separate fact at issue in the case, upon which two or more of the witnesses agree. That way, you can say, "Well, Charlie, Joe, and Sam all disagree as to the weather on the day in question, but Charlie and Sam both agree that the Plaintiff was not wearing his safety helmet when the accident occurred."

So, in summary, if you encounter conflicting testimony, here are some key strategies for dealing with it:

One: Acknowledge the conflicting testimony in your report. Don't wait for opposing counsel to throw it in your face;

Two: Look for, and present, supporting evidence and/or demonstrative evidence for the testimony of the witnesses. It is not enough to simply say you believe one over the other; you must offer supporting documentation for your opinion; and

Three: Look for, and present, any other issues about which two or more of the witnesses might agree; and then look for, and present, demonstrative evidence that supports their testimony. This potentially allows you to preserve the credibility of those witnesses, allowing you to use their testimony in your report.

• Seeing Your Report Through the Eyes of the Jury

First, I should mention that you will not necessarily be in front of a jury every time you are in a courtroom. Sometimes you will be at a bench trial—in front of only a judge.

It is often said in the legal community, and my personal experience confirms, you never know what a jury will consider to be important or not important. And, as I've mentioned previously in this book, it is also impossible to accurately predict how they will react to any set of facts, or circumstances. What may be very clear to me, you, or anyone else, may not be clear to that particular group of people.

Everything you do—from the way you construct and write your report, to your demeanor and appearance as you walk into a courtroom—is designed for one purpose: To convince the jury that the facts you've reviewed, and the opinions and conclusion you have drawn, are truthful, honest, convincing, and believable.

The most important thing to keep in mind with juries is that they are, by definition, comprised of lay people. As such, the jurors are unlikely to be the least bit familiar with the various aspects of your particular industry, business, or field of expertise. You must keep this in mind at all times: They don't do what you do for a living.

It is the expert's job to educate the trier of fact—the judge or jury. So, you need to express your opinions and conclusion in a clear and concise way that will make sense to the average man or woman.

Here's an example: I was recently following an online discussion among expert witnesses about plagiarism. An expert had a case whereby someone, in his opinion, plagiarized a series of documents.

Now, the expert in this matter is a math whiz, so to speak. He can recite mathematical formulas as long as your arm to prove probabilities of words repeating themselves between one document and another. Using those formulas, he could prove to within 93% probability that these documents were, in fact, the same, with only slight variations.

Here's the question he was posing to the discussion group: Would a jury be likely to understand the complex formula he had used to arrive at that percentage of probability? Or, was it better to simply say, "Here are three pages of this document, totaling 2,000 words. All but 106 of those words are exactly the same."

The consensus was that he should avoid going into complex formulas of probability, and keep it simple. Your goal, after all, is always the same—to make the jury comprehend what you are saying, in the simplest possible way.

• Calling a Spade a Spade

It is true that an expert should endeavor to be respectful, courteous, and professional at all times.

It is also true that, sometimes, you need to do what needs to be done—and that means calling a spade a spade. Or, to quote a line from the movie, *American President*, "Sometimes you just have to fight the fights that need fighting."

Of course, you, as an expert, will need to carefully choose those fights.

Here's an example of what I'm talking about: During deposition, an attorney once said, "So, Mr. Gulya, I see from your report in front of me that your fee is $285.00 per hour."

I said, "Yes, Counselor, that is my billable hourly rate."

He continued, "So, is it fair to say that you're being paid to testify, and effectively you're a hired gun?"

I said, "No, Counselor, I am being paid for my time; not the content of my testimony."

"But," he said, "you are in fact making a great deal of money here today!"

At this point, I said, "Yes—as you are getting paid to be here today!"

Now, I don't necessarily recommend giving this particular answer in all such instances. But, in this particular situation, opposing counsel was persistent in trying to imply that I was a hired gun that earns such a high fee, I would say anything to support retaining counsel's position.

This was a situation in which it was important to defuse the attorney's line of questioning, and render it ineffective. Or, to put it simply—to call a spade a spade.

• Going from Good to Great   *Law 30*

There are several qualities that separate a good expert from a great one: Discernment. Discretion. Finesse. Analytical dexterity. The ability to recognize those facts that stand out because they are more convincing than others.

The average expert takes a fact, repeats it, and forms opinions and a conclusion based upon it, without pointing out its true relevance and context. A great expert will take that same piece of evidence, and present it in such a way that its true weight can be felt—thereby grabbing the attention of the jury. It's not that the great expert is lying, twisting the truth, or embellishing it. He just knows how to best phrase—or present—his opinions and conclusion.

If you present your report in such a dry way that someone is going to fall asleep reading it, or the jury is going to become distracted listening to it, no one will ever get a sense of which evidence is most important. That's why, as discussed in an earlier section, I like to slowly build and build my report—and then really drive the point home with great force.

Another thing that sets a great expert apart from an average one is the willingness to recognize—and point out to retaining counsel—those facts in a case that are not necessarily most advantageous to the client's position.

The inexperienced expert will ignore those facts. And, that is a dangerous thing. The experienced expert is going to acknowledge such things, point them out to retaining counsel, and reference them in a subtle but truthful way in his report.

My previous discussion of three witnesses who each had a different version of the same situation was a classic example of this. Having three witnesses whose testimony differs can present a challenge.

The great expert will acknowledge the conflicting testimony, and use it to his advantage. He might say, "While there is conflicting testimony *on this one point*, the witnesses all agree that the plaintiff was wearing a seatbelt." This phrasing acknowledges the conflicting testimony—and defuses it at the same time, by pointing out what the witnesses *did* agree upon.

• Being Clear, Concise, and Instructive *Law 30*

I will never forget when I was about seventeen or eighteen, my father once said to me, "Listen, Bud (he always called me Bud), if that guy knew more than you, then you'd be asking *him* for advice!"

This was in the context of a conversation we were having with a client, who was asking a lot of questions about how we performed a certain aspect of our business—why we did something in a certain way, and in a particular sequence.

After the client finished asking us all these questions, he then started challenging the way we were planning to approach the job.

As my father and I left the meeting, I said to him, "Dad, I don't understand. This guy just grilled us to death about how we were going to do our job, and why we were going to do it that way. Then, after we'd explained it all to him, he questioned our reasoning behind doing it that way. If he knew so much, what was he doing asking us in the first place?"

That's when Dad said, "If that guy knew more than you, then you'd be asking *him* for advice!"

It is the same thing with expert work. You need to always keep in mind the fact that attorneys, judges, and especially juries, do not know as much about your particular field of expertise as you do. Your job as an expert is to educate them about your particular field. If you remain cognizant of that fact, then you will make sure every report is done in such a way as to be easy to understand and instructive, in terms of why you've formed particular opinions or conclusions.

If you're not clear, concise, and, mostly importantly, instructive, you run the danger of failing to get your opinions and conclusion across to the jury in a way they are going to understand. And, remember—what they don't understand, they are likely to discount, or fail to give the proper weight.

• Trusting Your Instincts   Law 29

In some ways, being an expert witness is like being a master chess player. You need to always be thinking a few moves ahead. This means that when an attorney is asking you a question, you need to be evaluating the question itself—*as well as the attorney's reason for asking it.*

You need to instinctively understand why an attorney is asking you a particular question or series of questions. You need to listen for the question *behind* the question. You need to sense where they are leading you, and what they are trying to accomplish.

Attorneys rarely ask you one question, and then sit down. It can happen, but it is not the norm. They are goal oriented, and will continue to question you along certain lines, until their goal is reached.

It is highly unusual that any one question will be that knife-in-the-heart type of question that will make or break their case. It is more common for them to try to dismantle your credibility, piece by piece, through a series of questions.

- ## Resisting the Temptation to Elaborate

Law 4

This brings me to another important issue. An expert should always answer only the question posed to them, and nothing more. Never volunteer information! The more information you volunteer, the more you provide opposing counsel with the ammunition he needs to shoot more questions your way.

Don't do opposing counsel's job for them. Just answer the question you are asked truthfully and clearly. There is no need to volunteer more information than the question requires. He or she will have plenty of opportunity to ask you more questions, if they wish.

- ## Avoiding the Appearance of Impropriety

You need to be cautious about how many times you agree to work for the same attorney.

Why? Is it illegal or unethical to repeatedly serve as an expert for the same attorney? Technically, no—but if a particular attorney continuously uses your services, it can *appear* that you are his hired gun.

Let's say you are retained as an expert by John Smith, Attorney at Law. You do the first case for him, and he's happy with your work. Then, several months later, Mr. Smith has another case in your field of expertise. So, once again, he retains you as an expert on the case.

Now, *you* know that you are always truthful, and base your opinions and conclusion on the facts of a case as presented to you. So, even if the same attorney hired you six consecutive times, you would not alter your opinion in his favor.

The thing you have to keep in mind is that such a scenario may give the *appearance of impropriety,* and you shouldn't dismiss that. As I've said repeatedly, appearances are important. And, perception is reality.

Here is the potential line of questioning from opposing counsel:

"Mr. Expert, can you tell the court how many times you have worked for Mr. Smith?"

"Yes, sir," you might reply, "I have worked for Mr. Smith six times."

"Six? Really?" At that point the attorney might pause, or look at the jury or judge for emphasis, before saying, "That seems like a high amount. He must really like you. Isn't it true that Mr. Smith gives you so much work, you will pretty much say anything he wants?"

You could respond to this line of questioning in such a way that you attempted to dispel any appearance of impropriety. And, the judge could issue an admonition to the jury about giving the attorney's line of questioning no weight. But, it wouldn't matter. This is exactly the sort of thing that the jury would pay attention to!

Does this mean you shouldn't work for the same attorney or law firm more than once? Not necessarily.

You could respond to that line of questioning by saying, "Counselor, I've worked for thirty different attorneys. I do not work exclusively for Mr. Smith. Additionally, Mr. Smith specializes in cases along my line of expertise, so, I would naturally be a good fit to opine. Furthermore, Counselor, I get paid for my time, not my opinion. Every case is different."

The moral is, you must remember that this line of questioning is likely to come your way when you have worked for the same attorney several times.

- **Being Prepared for Common Traps Set During Testimony**

  - **Trapped by the Date on Your Retainer Agreement**

When I'm retained by an attorney, I send out a retainer agreement, which we both sign and date. Attorneys will sometimes try to trap an expert using the date on the retainer agreement. Here's what can happen:

Opposing counsel may say, "I see that you've catalogued all the evidence very properly in your report.

I also see that you've properly noted the dates that you received that evidence. I can also see that your retainer agreement is dated prior to you receiving the evidence. Isn't that so?"

Such a question should never be answered with a yes or no.

What the attorney is trying to do here is imply that you agreed to testify, and formed opinions and a conclusion on the case, *before* you had an opportunity to study the evidence. It is a tactical ploy to discredit you.

This is a ridiculous strategy, considering that technically speaking, *every* expert agrees to testify based on an initial interview he has with retaining counsel. That does not mean the expert forms his opinions and/or conclusion before he considers the evidence. He does not!

In reality, my opinions and conclusion begin to form—or my suspicions begin to be confirmed or denied—as I begin to read the evidence. My opinions and conclusion *evolve* as I delve deeper into the evidence of the case.

When this tactic was used against me in a deposition, I answered the question as follows:

"Counselor, I agreed to evaluate the evidence, and provide my truthful opinions and conclusion based on that evidence. If you will notice, sir, my expert report, which contains my opinions and conclusion, is dated *six weeks after I received the last piece of evidence.*"

In order to understand the reason I answered that way, take a moment and picture yourself on a jury. The type of answer I just gave will help the jury immediately recognize that the attorney appears to be twisting the truth to unjustly score points with them.

Even if you are not in a jury setting, getting in the habit of answering such questions in this way will bolster credibility, while turning the tables on opposing counsel, and making him or her look less credible.

• Dismantling Your Credibility, Piece by Piece

A jury generally has no idea about the day-to-day machinations of the expert witness life. Attorneys bank on that fact—hoping that something they throw against the wall will stick, and the expert witness will be discredited, if only a little.

Take the example above, where opposing counsel used the date on an expert's retainer agreement to imply that the expert had formed his opinions and conclusion before examining the evidence. Remember, opposing attorneys want to chip away at your credibility, little by little. They will rarely try for one single, knockout blow—contrary to what you see on TV and in movies, where there's a sudden revelation, and the witness is made to look like a liar or an idiot.

Chipping away at you, piece by piece, is much more effective. That is what attorneys will be striving for—to catch you in little ambiguities in your statements or comments.

The first time it happens, and he points it out, it's no big deal. If he catches you again fifteen minutes later, it's still no big deal. But, if he catches you *again and again*, he can take all the little things he's chipped away at, and drop the hammer on you. This happens during the courtroom summaries you see on TV—those big climactic scenes:

"So, Mr. Expert, we talked about A, and you said B—and that wasn't correct. And we talked about C, and you said D, and that wasn't right, either. Then we talked about X, Y, and Z, and you recanted your testimony! What else would you like to recant?"

At the end of the day—and, I mean literally, at the end of the day of testimony—all those little things add up, and become a much bigger thing.

• Getting You to Qualify Their Witness

During a trial, an attorney once asked me, "Did you read the expert witness report of the plaintiff?"

I answered, "Yes. Thoroughly."

He continued, "Did you find his qualifications satisfactory and acceptable?"

This sounds like an innocuous enough question, doesn't it? You can be assured that it is not. The attorney was trying to get me to assist him in qualifying his witness.

"Well, Counselor," I said, "it is not my place to qualify your witness."

He said, "Sir you are an expert! You must have some opinion of the plaintiff's expert."

I replied, "Counselor, I have not formed any opinion of your expert's qualifications."

He persisted, "If you *had* a negative opinion, you certainly would express it wouldn't you?"

I said, "Counselor, it is up to the court to determine if your expert is qualified in his field of expertise. It is not my place."

The attorney would not drop his line of questioning. He went on, saying, "But, sir his expertise is in the same field as yours. You must have an opinion!"

At that point, retaining counsel jumped in and said, "Your Honor, I object! Asked and answered several times. Counsel is badgering the witness, clearly asking for an opinion that it is not his place to provide. He is not an attorney, and, as the court knows, acceptance or rejection of an expert is for the court to decide."

The judge sustained the objection.

Opposing counsel was trying to gain two things in that exchange. First, he was trying to get me to agree that his expert was qualified—and if he got lucky, maybe he could even get me to imply that his witness was highly regarded in some way.

I understood what he was doing, and refused to play into his hand. It was not my place to qualify any other expert, or express my opinion of their competence.

- **Getting You to Admit That Your Testimony is Rehearsed**

During deposition, opposing counsel asked me, "Did you and the retaining counsel discuss this case in preparation for this deposition?"

Remember when I said that one of the previous questions seemed innocuous, but it wasn't? Well, this question seems ominous, but it isn't.

It is expected that you will discuss the case with retaining counsel prior to deposition. Just tell the truth, and admit it.

In one instance, I was asked this question and responded, "Yes, we met for a couple of hours to review the case just the other day."

The attorney then continued by asking me, "Isn't it a fact that you met for several days with the retaining counsel?"

I answered honestly, "Yes, we did meet on several different occasions; it is a detailed case with thousands of pages of evidence."

He then asked, "Is it true that the retaining counselor discussed what questions he would ask during direct examination?"

I explained, "We reviewed my report, and discussed my testimony, as you likely did with your expert."

The attorney then tried to twist my words. He said, "So, he discussed how you should answer the questions, isn't that right?"

I stated, "No, sir, but he did say to stick to the facts and tell the truth."

In cases like this, the opposing counsel is trying to hammer a point to the jury, in an attempt to convince them that your testimony is rehearsed. He is trying to limit, or reduce, your credibility. The answers I provided neutralize this tactic.

As always, tell the truth. It is expected that you will discuss and review the case with retaining counsel, and it is perfectly acceptable for you to do so.

• Interrupting Your Testimony

I was in the process of answering a direct question during cross-examination. The question required more than a brief answer. I broke eye contact with the attorney, and turned toward the jury to continue my answer.

In the middle of my answer, the attorney interrupted me.

I weighed my options. Was it better to stop speaking, and remain quiet? Or, keep talking, and ignore the attorney's interruption?

I chose to keep talking, and finished my answer, despite opposing counsel's repeated interruptions of, "Mr. Expert, Mr. Expert!"

Continuing with your answer while opposing counsel is attempting to interrupt you can be very effective. The jury may perceive that opposing counsel is trying to prevent them from hearing expert testimony damaging to his case. The jury will observe opposing counsel's desperation to get you to stop answering the question.

Under such circumstances, the jury tends to pay more attention to the answer being provided.

Remember—your goal is to tell the truth, and convey it to the jury. If you are stopped by the judge, respectfully request that you be allowed to complete your answer. Under all circumstances, obey the judge's ruling.

- **Putting Words in Your Mouth**

In deposition, I was asked, "Is it fair to say that Mr. X was a trained operator?"

The attorney was trying to put words in my mouth.

I answered, "No, Sir. What I said was that his training was limited to only ten hours on the backhoe he was operating at the time of the accident."

The attorney continued, "Well, is it fair to say that ten hours is the standard training time?"

He thus provided me with an opportunity to state my opinion definitively, and drive it home to the jury. I said, "Counselor, ten hours of training is woefully inadequate to learn how to safely operate any large piece of heavy construction equipment."

*Never allow opposing counsel to misquote you, or put words in your mouth.

• Trying to Limit Your Answers to Yes or No

I was asked in deposition, "Was the shoring up to the exact OSHA standards—yes or no?"

I said, "Let me explain."

The attorney cut me off, saying, "Sir, it is a simple question that only requires a yes or no answer."

I said, "Counselor, it is a complex matter."

He persisted, saying, "For the last time, please answer the question!"

I replied, "Counselor, your question is oversimplifying the matter."

At that point, opposing counsel turned to the judge and said, "Your Honor, please instruct the witness to answer the question. It only requires a simple yes or no answer." Opposing counsel was trying to make a complex matter simple, to suit his needs.

The judge then turned to me and asked, "Can you answer the question with a yes or no answer?"

I responded as follows: "Your Honor, I cannot honestly and truthfully answer with a simple yes or no."

The judge instructed me to "answer the question truthfully and honestly."

If you are ever in such a position, stand your ground, politely and professionally. Don't get nervous. Maintain your composure. The tone of your voice should not be argumentative, but mild-mannered.

The judge wants the truth to be told, and will, therefore, in most circumstances, allow you to expand on your answer.

• Taking Your Report Out of Context

On a certain case, opposing counsel was taking a section of my report out of context.

In my report, I had stated, "The third party rental rates, when compared against industry standards, were found to be on the higher end of the national range charged by major heavy equipment rental firms."

My statement about the third party rental rates *did not end there, however.* I went on to explain in greater detail in the following paragraph.

The attorney, however, ignored what I'd written in the following paragraph, and asked me, "So, Mr. Gulya, you acknowledged that the third party rental rates were higher than average?"

So, I asked him, "Where in my report are you exactly referring to?"

When he directed me to page 20, paragraph R, I asked to see the report. He handed it to me, and I took a moment to read the preceding paragraph, the paragraph in question, and the following paragraph.

Afterwards, I said, "Counselor, you are taking my statement out of context. What I said was that 'the price was on the higher end of the national range.' In addition, in the following paragraph, I stated that, adjusting for published state cost variances, the rental rates were within average range for the State of California."

*An expert should always challenge opposing counsel if you believe your statements have been taken out of context. Always ask to read the report. Be sure to read no less than the preceding and the subsequent paragraphs, to confirm or deny your suspicion.

• Using Your Own Words Against You

Even the very best expert witnesses occasionally make a poor choice of words when writing their report. We are only human, after all.

In one of my reports, I wrote, "I believe the equipment was in disrepair, and the swing-piston bushings were worn, causing excessive slop or movement in the boom."

During cross-examination, opposing counsel jumped on this, asking me, "You stated *you believe* the equipment was in disrepair, and the swing-piston bushings were worn, causing excessive and uncontrollable movement in the boom. Is that correct?"

I instantly recognized my poor choice of the words "I believe" and seized the opportunity to rephrase what I had written.

I said, "Yes. It is my opinion, *to a reasonable degree of professional certainty,* that the swing-piston bushings were worn out, causing excessive and uncontrollable movement in the boom."

*Whenever you recognize a poor choice of words you have used, it is important to adjust it through testimony, as I did in this case.

By correcting this oversight, I blocked and prevented an entire line of questioning. Had I just answered yes, the attorney would have stated, "So you *believe* they were worn out, but you aren't sure." And, he would have then moved right on to another question, having succeeded in planting doubt in the jurors' minds as to the accuracy or certainty of my opinion. (You often see this sort of dialogue in TV shows and movies.)

Notice that, in the above example, the attorney *stated*, "So you believe, but you're not sure." He didn't *ask*, "Oh, so you believe, but you're not sure. Isn't that true?" One approach leaves an opening for you to redeem yourself. The other does not.

You may one day find yourself in a similar position. If an attorney tries to shut you down by making a statement, rather than asking you a question, and you have no opportunity to respond, don't panic. Remember, retaining counsel has most certainly made a note of this, and will rectify it during redirect.

It is best, of course, never to let it get to that point, if you can help it. Whenever possible, it is much better to turn things around early during the initial question, by recognizing your poor choice or words, and correcting or clarifying it with your testimony.

- **Knowing The Definition and Meaning of Legal Terms**

I was retained on a case involving proof of negligence. In deposition, I was asked this question: "You state in your report that, to a reasonable degree of certainty, the defendant was negligent. Is that correct?"

I said, "Yes, Sir."

The attorney then said, "Negligence is a legal term. Can you list the four basic elements of negligence?"

I replied, "Yes, Sir. The four basic elements of negligence are duty, breach, causation, and damages."

If you're going to use a term like negligence—which is, by and large, a legal term—it is vital to know the legal definition and meaning.

Had I not been able to provide opposing counsel with the four basic elements of negligence, he would have undoubtedly said, "Mr. Gulya, you want this jury to believe that my client was negligent, yet you don't even know the four basic elements of negligence!"

I would have looked incompetent, and lost a great deal of credibility in the eyes of the jury.

If you are going to use any legal phrase or verbiage, be sure you know their definition and meaning.

- **Understanding the Definition of Negligence**

Depending upon your field of expertise, you may also need to know the definition of negligence and gross negligence—and understand the difference between a common definition and a legal definition.

Many cases related to construction fall under the category of personal injury, and many of those cases involve the *legal* definition of either negligence or gross negligence.

The common definition is not necessarily the legal one, and it's important to know the distinction. Jurors will be read the legal definition, and attorneys will discuss the common definition in open court. While they are similar, they are not the same.

The common definition of negligence is generally defined as, "Conduct that is culpable because it falls short of what a reasonable person would do to protect another individual from foreseeable risk or harm."

The legal definition, on the other hand, goes beyond mere carelessness: "Someone might exercise as much care as they are capable of, yet still fall far below the level of competence expected of them. They could also be aware of issues, *yet choose to put the issues aside because they underestimated the importance of those issues.*" (Emphasis added.)

If you went only by the common definition, there might be too much ambiguity. So, as an expert, you need to consider the subtle differences between the common definition and the legal definition.

In my opinion, the major difference is the sentence that states, "They could also be aware of issues, yet choose to put the issues aside because they underestimated the importance of those issues."

Here is what this means, in plain language: A contractor might decide that orange cones are sufficient to prevent someone from walking into a trench they have dug; and a fence, barrier, or barricade (such as a forty-two-inch-high safety railing) is not necessary. (See the Noteworthy Cases chapter for the discussion of that case.)

The common definition would not take into account the fact that because the contractor didn't think something was important, he didn't bother to do it.

When I first began practicing as an expert witness, I didn't think twice about the definitions of negligence or gross negligence. I figured, *Well, an expert is not a lawyer and not expected to be proficient in the law.*

Nothing could be further from the truth! In reality, an expert *does* need to know, and understand, the principles of law that would apply to whatever case they have been retained to opine on.

During an attorney interview, counsel might say to me, "Listen, this is a clear case of negligence."

Boom! Big alarm bells go off. Right away, I know they may be pointing at negligence. On the other hand, the attorney might simply mean that Party A was harmed or damaged in some way by Party B's carelessness (negligence), rather than by Party B's knowledge that a clear and present danger existed (gross negligence).

If I didn't have a full understanding of negligence, I would not know that negligence could arise because someone was aware of an issue, but chose to set aside that issue because they underestimated its importance.

Let's say I'm reading a piece of evidence stating that a contractor put up cones every three feet around an open trench, and believed that to be an adequate safety measure—and a woman walked into the trench, the perimeter of which was lined with orange cones (see the Noteworthy Cases chapter for the discussion of that case).

I might think, *Well, they did put up the orange cones as a safety measure. But, was that enough, according to industry standards?*

Understanding the *legal* definition of negligence, and considering it along with the other evidence, I would see that they might have set aside, or underestimated, the importance of having a forty-two-inch-high safety railing or something equivalent to it.

• Understanding Gross Negligence

In contrast to negligence, gross negligence requires an additional burden of proof. It is defined as: "Conscious and voluntary disregard of the need to use reasonable care, which is likely to cause foreseeable grave injury or harm to persons, property, or both."

Gross negligence implies extreme conduct—and, unlike simple negligence, it implies intent. It comes down to someone *knowingly* doing something that is likely to cause harm or injury to persons or property, or both.

Let's say someone got into their car, knowing the brakes didn't work, and went driving down the road, and hit a person or someone's property. That is something they did, knowingly and voluntarily, that ultimately caused harm to person or property. They knew they shouldn't have gotten behind the wheel of the car. They knew something bad was likely to happen if they did. But, they didn't give a damn.

An attorney does not choose whether they are

going to attempt to prove simple negligence or gross negligence. Considering the extra burden of proof associated with gross negligence, no attorney would voluntarily elect to meet that stricter burden. But, there will be times when the circumstances of the case dictate that they must prove gross negligence.

- **Using the Legal Definition in its Proper Order**

An expert needs to consider the following things in their proper order:
First—best practices and industry standards;
Secondly—the evidence; and
Third—the legal definition applicable to the case on which you've been retained.

Yes, experts deal with best practices and industry standards. Yes, they deal with evidence. And, yes, they also need to understand the legal definition (of negligence, for example) as it applies to the evidence. This is important because the definition may highlight the importance of particular evidence—which is then magnified by the supporting best practices and industry standards you apply to it.

So, those three elements must be applied in the order mentioned above.

Plainly put, your comprehension of the legal definition becomes like a magnifying glass through which to view the evidence, in order to see which evidence appears most prominent. Having done so, you then lay down the magnifying glass, and give your opinion based upon best practices and industry standards.

• Surviving Motions to Disqualify You as an Expert

No matter how prepared you may be, or how experienced you become, once in awhile, something you couldn't possibly have anticipated will take you totally by surprise. This happened to me recently.

I was retained to opine on a case related to heavy equipment rental—and then the attorney who retained me was fired by the principal of the equipment rental company. When an attorney that hires me is fired by his client, I am out of a job. This was an unexpected turn of events, but the big surprise was yet to come.

The principal of the equipment rental company and I had a good relationship. So, when he found a new attorney to represent him in a new dispute, he wanted to bring me in as an expert witness on the case.

I told him, "Listen, Steve, I would love to do this for you. But, if you want your new attorney to retain me, I'll need a new, signed retainer agreement and payment."

Over the next several months, we went back and forth with correspondence and phone calls. I kept reminding both the client and his new attorney that I needed the signed agreement and payment if they planned to retain me. They kept promising they'd send them, but never did.

Finally, I got a call from Steve. "Well, Bill, we are going to court in a couple of weeks."

I said, "I'm sorry to hear you weren't able to settle it. What can I do for you?"

He explained that they were going to need me to testify in court—and I reminded him, once again, that I could not do anything on his behalf until I received a signed agreement and retainer payment.

"We will take care of it…but, Bill, there's one little hiccup. The opposition made a motion to the court to disqualify you as an expert!"

I was stunned! As of the date of this writing, that was the one and only time I have ever been challenged.

I asked him, "What grounds could they possibly have for trying to disqualify me? Do you happen to know what terminology or language they used in the motion?"

He didn't know the details. So, I placed a call to his attorney, who told me that the opposition had indeed filed a motion to disqualify me, and he had filed a response. He explained, "Their argument was weak. Mostly, they were just taking pot-shots at you. I sincerely doubt that the court will take their motion seriously, and deny you, especially at this stage of the game."

I couldn't take his reassurances to the bank. You never know *what* the court will do.

Before we hung up, the attorney said, "Let's wait and see what happens. We'll let you know, based on the outcome, whether or not we need you to appear."

Naturally, I was curious about the basis for the motion to disqualify me—but I wasn't kept wondering for long. Within a few days of my conversation with the attorney, I received an email from him, stating, "The court has denied the motion to exclude you. We'll talk soon."

I was relieved to know that the motion had been denied. And since it was denied, I no longer felt the need to know the opposition's grounds for trying to exclude me. The fact that the motion *was denied* told me everything I needed to know: There was no valid basis for trying to exclude me.

We have all heard the childhood rhyme, "Sticks and stones may break my bones, but names will never hurt me." Any motion to disqualify an expert witness that does not result in disqualification is nothing more than name-calling, and should not unduly affect me—or you!

Closing Argument

Every career has its upsides and downsides. As I have illustrated throughout this book, being an expert witness is no exception.

It can be lucrative. It can be exhilarating. It can also be nerve wracking, pressure packed, and emotional.

Reading thousands of pages of evidence can seem overwhelming; exhausting, even. Writing an expert report, and making sure to dot every *i* and cross every *t*, can seem intimidating. Testifying at depositions and in formal courtrooms, and having attorney after attorney grill you with question after question, can be mentally fatiguing.

So why in the world did I decide to take on this type of vocation?

I chose to do it because I wanted to make a difference. I wanted to use my vast experience and knowledge to help guide justice to the truth, and make a difference in people's lives. It was a calling of sorts— similar, perhaps, to what might be felt by a teacher who takes pleasure in, and receives gratification from, educating our youth.

You will have—or you will find —your own reasons, whatever they may be. Take my experience and knowledge sprinkled throughout this book. Study it, understand it, and apply it. Serve your client to the best of your ability.

I can assure you that, despite all the ups and downs, being an expert witness is truly gratifying.

And remember—if you tell the truth, the whole truth, and nothing but the truth, while applying your knowledge and expertise, you really *will* make a difference!

Resources

Babitsky, S., Esq., & Mangraviti, J. J., Jr. (2006). *The A to Z Guide to Expert Witnessing* . 2006: SEAK, Inc. (Original work published 2006)

Babitsky, S., Esq., & Mangraviti, J. J., Jr. (2008). *How Expert Witnesses Can Excel During the Initial Inquiry Call from Counsel* . Seak Inc. (Original work published 2008)

Babitsky, S., Esq., & Mangraviti, J. J., Jr. Esq. (2002). *Writing and Defending Your Expert Report, The Step-By-Step Guide with Models* (2nd ed.). Seak. (Original work published 2002)

Erickson, B. (n.d.). *Speech style and impression formation in a court setting : the effects of "power" and "power-less" speech.* Durham, N.C.Law and Language Program. (Original work published 1977). doi:60887135

Gunn, L. (Speaker). (n.d.). *How to Be Picked, But Not Picked Apart* [CD].

Hamilton, R. (2003). *The Expert Witness Marketing Book, How to Promote Your Forensic Practice in a Professional and Cost-effective Manner.* Author. (Original work published 2003)

Poynter, D. (2005). *The expert Witness Handbook Tips and Techniques for the Litigation Consultant* (3rd ed.). Santa Barbara California: Para Publishing. (Original work published 1997)

Vulkelic, J. M. (2005). *Testifying Under Oath, How to Be an Effective Witness*. Volcano California: Volcano Press. (Original work published 2005)

Disclaimer:

Every effort has been taken to give credit where credit is due. I apologize for any inadvertent omission of any particular item or resource in the Resources or Acknowledgements sections. Please email Resource and or Acknowledgement recommendations to wgulya@siteworkexpert.com The oversight will be corrected, and will be added at the next book printing.

CPSIA information can be obtained at www.ICGtesting.com
Printed in the USA
LVOW10s2330141113

361382LV00002B/2/P